j629.4 M167s
The space adventurer's
guide :your passport to the
coolest things to
McMahon, Peter,   AUG 0 4 2018

WITHDRAWN

The Space
ADVENTURER'S
Guide

D1122685

For my wife, Kristina, my favorite adventure companion in all the universe — P.M.

There's no point in being mean to anyone when you consider how big the universe is — J.H.

Acknowledgments

Space is complex and our knowledge of it is changing all the time. While numerous astronomers and engineers were consulted for this book, three people deserve credit above all: author and space tourism expert John Spencer who helped me turn this book into a wonderful set of adventures, both possible and soon-could-be possible; former Boeing and SpaceX engineer Daniel Villani, who was the guy I talked to when I needed to ask if an idea or concept I wanted to write about was realistic, and whose support and encouragement kept me believing in a book about going to space for fun; and finally I'd like to thank Kids Can Press editor Stacey Roderick for her constant patience and eye for detail, which has helped create a book that's fun to read and inspiring for the next generation of space explorers.

Text © 2018 Peter McMahon
Illustrations © 2018 Josh Holinaty

All rights reserved. No part of this publication may be reproduced, stored in a retrieval system or transmitted, in any form or by any means, without the prior written permission of Kids Can Press Ltd. or, in case of photocopying or other reprographic copying, a license from The Canadian Copyright Licensing Agency (Access Copyright). For an Access Copyright license, visit www.accesscopyright.ca or call toll free to 1-800-893-5777.

Many of the designations used by manufacturers and sellers to distinguish their products are claimed as trademarks. Where those designations appear in this book and Kids Can Press Ltd. was aware of a trademark claim, the designations have been printed in initial capital letters (e.g., Lego).

Kids Can Press gratefully acknowledges the financial support of the Government of Ontario, through the Ontario Media Development Corporation; the Ontario Arts Council; the Canada Council for the Arts; and the Government of Canada, through the CBF, for our publishing activity.

Published in Canada and the U.S. by Kids Can Press Ltd.
25 Dockside Drive, Toronto, ON M5A 0B5

Kids Can Press is a Corus Entertainment Inc. company

www.kidscanpress.com

The artwork in this book was rendered in Photoshop.
The text is set in Conflict.

Edited by Stacey Roderick
Designed by Marie Bartholomew

Printed and bound in Shenzhen, China, in 10/2017 through Asia Pacific Offset

CM 18 0 9 8 7 6 5 4 3 2 1

Library and Archives Canada Cataloguing in Publication

McMahon, Peter, 1977–, author
   The space adventurer's guide : your passport to the coolest things to see and do in the universe / written by Peter McMahon ; illustrated by Josh Holinaty.

Includes index.
ISBN 978-1-77138-032-4 (softcover)

   1. Astronautics — Juvenile literature. 2. Outer space — Juvenile literature.
3. Outer space — Exploration — Juvenile literature. 4. Space tourism — Juvenile literature.
I. Holinaty, Josh, illustrator II. Title.

TL793.M348 2018   j629.4   C2017-904612-8

The Space ADVENTURER'S Guide

YOUR PASSPORT TO THE COOLEST THINGS TO SEE AND DO IN THE UNIVERSE

Peter McMahon • Josh Holinaty

Kids Can Press

Astronaut James Newman waves at the camera during a space walk outside the Unity Module of the International Space Station.

CONTENTS

So ... You Want to Go to SPACE?   6

SUBORBIT: Surfboard Spaceships and Giant-Panda G-FORCES   18

EARTH ORBIT: Around the World in 90 MINUTES   28

ORBITAL CRUISE: All Aboard Your SPACE YACHT   38

The MOON: Crater Skiing and BAMBOO HOTELS   48

COMETS: Discovering Your Own SPACE SNOWBALL   58

MARS: A Journey to the RED PLANET   66

JUPITER: A Solar System Within a SOLAR SYSTEM   76

SATURN: A Frozen PARADISE   84

What's Next? TO THE STARS!   94

INDEX   97

So...You Want to Go to SPACE?

Have you ever looked up at the stars and wondered what's out there? For the first few decades of spaceflight, vacationing in the cosmos was something that only happened in science fiction.

But now, journeys into space are becoming more possible for more people. And that means, with some preparation and a taste for adventure, one of those people could be *you*.

Trip of a Lifetime

Getting to take a trip into space used to mean that you had to be at the top of your class in math, science and lots of other subjects. After that, you'd have to become one of the best fighter pilots in the world or be an incredible scientist. Speaking several languages and being really good at sports and different hobbies would also help. But even with all these qualities, you and thousands of others would still have had to compete for only a handful of professional astronaut jobs.

While doing well in school is always a good idea and getting paid to explore the cosmos would be pretty awesome, the exciting news is that there are now more opportunities to become a space adventurer. Today, the dream of heading to space isn't just for those who work for government organizations like the National Aeronautics and Space Administration (NASA) or the Canadian Space Agency (CSA).

Already, a small number of people have gone on vacations using spaceships originally built for astronauts working in space. Meanwhile, the development of new materials means engineers are working to build more efficient spacecraft for quick trips into space for fun and adventure. New ways of thinking have created plans for "space cruisers"

Astronaut Tracy Caldwell Dyson looks out a window in the Cupola of the International Space Station. A part of Earth and the blackness of space can be seen through the windows.

to take vacationers to the Moon and other places near the Earth. And new technology being developed right now could mean travel to destinations like Mars, the moons of Jupiter and beyond.

Going into space for fun has actually been possible for a while. The first paying space tourist went up way back in 2001, when an American businessman named Dennis Tito took a one-week vacation in Earth orbit at the International Space Station (ISS). But it was expensive — he had to pay U.S. $20 million for the experience. Since then, a total of seven people (including former Microsoft executive Charles Simonyi and Cirque du Soleil co-founder Guy Laliberté) have vacationed on the ISS.

As well, hundreds of people have trips booked on rockets that fly shorter suborbital trips (roughly 100 km [60 mi.] above the Earth). But at U.S. $95 000 to $250 000 a ticket, that's still a lot of pocket change for the average person. Once more people have gone, though, experts predict that the cost of taking a space vacation could drop down to the average price of a new car.

Training for Your Space Vacation

Though you won't have to train as hard as a professional astronaut for your trip into the universe, there are still things you'll need to learn and do as an aspiring space traveler.

To spend any amount of time in space, you'll need to be in good physical shape. It's important to exercise (to build up your muscle strength and endurance) and eat well leading up to the trip. You'll also be given a medical checkup to make sure you don't have any serious health conditions that would make space travel too dangerous.

For a suborbital trip, you'll actually be in space for only a few minutes. So after passing the physical exam, you'll likely take some practice runs in a spinning centrifuge to get used to the extreme forces you'll experience on your flight. (You'll read more about this kind of flight simulator later but for now, just imagine being strapped inside a giant spinning top.)

Training for trips to the worlds beyond Earth orbit, however, is a bit different.

For these longer trips, your training will also be longer — months or even more. You'll need to become an expert on everything from aeronautics (the science of air travel) and learning how to deal with medical and other emergencies, to the more day-to-day stuff, such as repairing the toilet (which could also be considered a type of emergency) and cutting your fellow passengers' hair.

You'll also have to get used to living with others in small spaces (possibly as small as a moving van), drinking liquids and eating food out of bags, working on a day-night schedule different from that of Earth, and locking yourself in a tiny radiation shelter (a thick-walled room that protects you) every time the sun burps out a solar flare in your direction.

(Top right): Restrained by a harness, astronaut Guion Bluford exercises on the treadmill on the space shuttle Challenger.

(Center right): Commander Richard Truly sleeps right-side up, while astronaut Guion Bluford sleeps upside down on the space shuttle Challenger.

(Bottom right): Space food — bags of snack foods and dehydrated foods.

(Below): STS-131 and Expedition 23 crew members pose for a photo on the International Space Station. STS-131 crew members are pictured in the light blue shirts, while the Expedition 23 crew are wearing darker shirts.

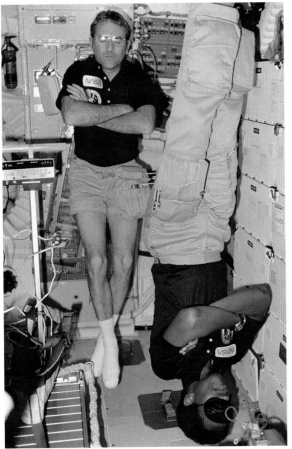

Have some time before your trip? Consider enrolling in a "space camp" like those offered at science centers and space agencies around the world. There, you'll get to experience what it's like to plan a mission, train for it, serve as a mission-control member and use some simulators to experience a few of the sensations you'd feel flying in a spaceship.

You might be surprised to find out that the gravitational pull of the Earth is nearly the same hundreds of kilometers (or miles) above our planet as it is on its surface. But as a space traveler in Earth orbit, you'll get to feel the sensation of weightlessness while your spacecraft is "falling" around Earth fast enough to cancel most of gravity's influence. (Actually, there is still a tiny amount of gravity — called "microgravity" — that varies a little depending on where you are in your spacecraft.) But beyond the orbit of the Moon, the gravitational pull from the planets and their moons is much, much less. In fact, you could think of this space between planets (and beyond) as having zero gravity.

Getting Ready for the Greatest Show *Off* Earth

Simulations are among the most useful tools for space training. Whether it's a computer program or a full-scale model spaceship, a simulation is designed to imitate elements of your space adventure. Simulations help you gain experience without posing real-world danger.

To prepare for the sensation of weightlessness, one kind of zero-gravity simulation happens inside a specially modified passenger jet with an empty, padded area in place of the plane's usual seats.

Using current rocket technology:
- a trip to the Moon and back will take days
- a trip to a comet will take anywhere from one to four years depending on how far it is from Earth
- to get to the planets of the inner solar system (such as Venus or Mars) and back will take months or even years (depending on the distance between the planet and Earth at the time of the trip)
- a journey to the planets of the outer solar system (such as Jupiter or Saturn) and back could take up to ten years

These "vomit comets" (you can guess how they got this nickname) climb as fast as they can up to an altitude (height above the ground) of about the same as a typical airplane flight. As the plane gets close to its maximum altitude, you start to feel lighter and lighter. Finally, your feet, arms and then your whole body rise off the floor to float in mid-air for 20 to 30 seconds. Then the plane dives downward to its starting altitude before leveling out for its next run. During a session of zero-gravity training, you'll get to do this about a dozen times.

Another way you might train for the feeling of weightlessness is to jump into a giant, specially designed pool of water. Weights will be attached to you so that you neither float up to the surface nor sink down to the bottom — instead, you hover in place like an astronaut in space. NASA runs the world's largest underwater training facility, which is 60 m (200 ft.) long and 12 m (40 ft.) deep and is used to train astronauts for space walks.

(Above): Zero-G's Airbus A300 climbing toward a weightlessness simulation.

(Below): Astronauts Rick Mastracchio (left) and Koichi Wakata (right) train for a space walk in the waters of NASA's Neutral Buoyancy Lab (NBL).

Once you've trained for a lack of gravity, it's time to prepare for the *additional* gravity you'll experience during launch and upon your return.

Why would you need to train for this? The ship's rapid acceleration (increased speed) causes g-forces to build up and pile on several times more weight than the gravity you're used to. (You and your body are used to living in 1g — a "g" is equal to normal gravity on the surface of the Earth.) You can experience dozens of gs for a split second without suffering any real damage, but if you were to undergo as little as 5 gs for more than a minute, you could pass out.

To prepare for these extra gs, you'll need g-force training ... which might not be as fun as it sounds. In a high-g simulator, you'll spend a few minutes at a time strapped into a seat inside a sealed capsule at the end of a giant centrifuge arm, swinging around at the speed of a car on the highway.

As well as spending time in the high-g simulator, you'll also need to practice exercises that help you tolerate more gs, such as flexing your arm and leg muscles and controlling your breathing.

After several days of getting used to high g-forces (don't worry — you won't be spinning around in the centrifuge the whole time), it's a good idea to try out a machine that can simulate both the movements your ship might make *and* extra g-forces.

One option is to take a high-altitude flight in a military fighter jet, which is almost like going on a suborbital trip. Or, some of today's space tourism companies use copies of the insides of their spaceships built inside real aircraft. For example, Virgin Galactic has a SpaceShipTwo suborbital craft replica built inside its WhiteKnightTwo jet. That way, before actually going up into space, you can fly around and get used to the motions space adventurers will feel during a trip to or from space.

The 20-G Centrifuge at the Ames Research Center can produce forces up to 20 times that of terrestrial gravity.

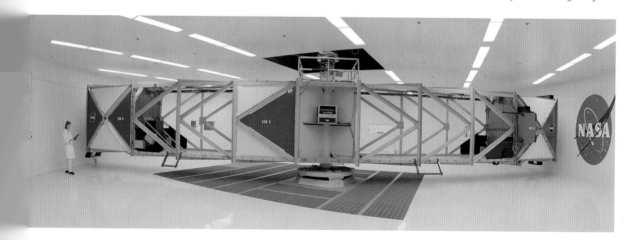

The 37-million horsepower main engines of a space shuttle fire just before liftoff.

G-Suits for Super-G-Forces

High g-forces can force blood away from important parts of your body, such as your head and chest, causing you to faint, get seriously injured or, in extreme cases, die. During some of your final pre-space simulations, you may get to wear a g-suit — a kind of anti-g-force jumpsuit. G-suits have special sacs that inflate to press on different parts of your body, keeping blood from draining the wrong way when g-forces increase.

Today's g-suits take up to two seconds to inflate. That means that you're still going to feel some of the effects of the g-forces when your craft launches, makes a hard turn or slows quickly. Next-generation g-suits being perfected for future flights will inflate almost instantly.

From the intense vibrations you'll feel at the start of a space shuttle launch, to the violent movements of a space capsule as it enters the atmosphere, and all the way to the extreme gravity you may experience along the way, you'll be glad you trained well for your upcoming space adventure.

There's a test you can take to see how you'll react to your return to gravity after a trip in space. For this "tilt test," you're strapped to a special table lying down and then quickly tilted upward into a standing position. Believe it or not, this helps to see how likely it is you'll faint from the rapid changes in position upon your return. But don't try this at home!

3... 2 ...1... BLAST OFF!

Once you've trained for your trip, you'll be ready for the real deal: the face-rearranging g-forces of launch and re-entry; the freedom of floating weightless; the challenge of catching food in your mouth while coasting through the air like a bird ...

So, if you could fly anywhere in the cosmos, where would you want to go?

On Earth we have amazing sights such as Egypt's Great Pyramid of Giza and the ancient mountain ridge city of Machu Picchu in Peru. Ever thought about what the cosmic version of the Wonders of the World might be? Here are just a few of the spectacular space adventurer must-sees you can discover throughout this guide:

▶ The Grand Canyon from suborbit
— *see more on pages 36–37*

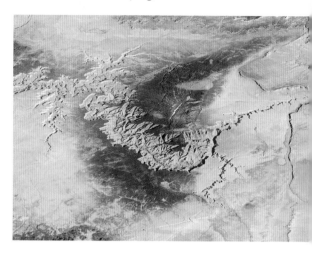

▶ Australia's Great Barrier Reef from orbit
— *see more on page 34*

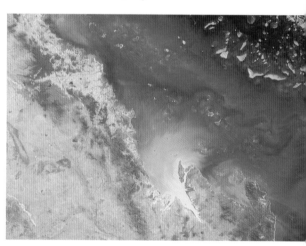

▶ The Northern Lights from orbit
— *see more on page 34*

▶ The Moon's Tycho Crater
  — *see more on page 43*

▶ Mar's Olympus Mons
  — *see more on pages 72–73 and 75*

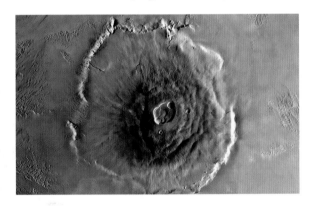

▶ The 400 volcanoes of Io (one of the
  moons of Jupiter)
  — *see more on pages 81 and 82*

▶ The lakes of Titan (one of Saturn's
  moons) — *see more on pages 91 and 92*

▶ The tail of a comet at close range
  — *see more on pages 58, 59, 63 and 65*

It would take a long time to visit all these wonders (after all, scientists and engineers are still in the planning stages for some of these trips), but maybe you'll take a cosmic vacation to one or more of these places in your not-too-distant future.

Learn to Speak "Astronaut"

To prepare for any out-of-this world journey, you'll need to know some specialized space lingo.

altitude: the height above ground

asteroid: an object (smaller than a planet) made of rock and metal that orbits a star

astronaut: a professional trained to participate in spaceflight

atmosphere: the layer of gases surrounding a planet, moon or other large object in space

aurora: the colorful lights that appear over the north and south poles of Earth and other planets. Sometimes called the Northern Lights (and Southern Lights), auroras occur when solar wind particles collide with particles in a planet's magnetic field.

centrifuge: a motorized device that rotates an object or person around a fixed point. The faster the rotation, the more force felt by that object or person.

comet: a large ball of ice and rock. When a comet gets close enough to the Sun, heat turns the ice into gas, which erupts to form a tail hundreds of thousands of kilometers (or miles) long or more.

cosmos: the universe and anything that might lie beyond it

flyby: a spacecraft's flight past a planet or other body in space

galaxy: a collection of dust, gas and billions (or even trillions) of stars. There are probably about 2 trillion galaxies or more in the universe. Our galaxy is called the Milky Way.

g-force: a measure of the effects of gravity or acceleration

gravity: the attracting force between objects. The Earth's gravity causes objects to fall to the ground. The pull of gravity is also what causes a planet to orbit a star or a moon to orbit a planet.

g-suit: a piece of clothing that helps decrease the force of extra gravity (higher than that felt on Earth) on a person

meteor: a meteoroid that has entered a planet's atmosphere

meteorite: a meteor that has landed on another solar system body, such as on Earth

meteoroid: a small rocky or metallic body in space

microgravity: the near-zero gravity in which objects (and people) seem weightless

Moon: the name of the natural satellite that orbits Earth. The satellites of other planets are often also called moons.

mother ship: a large space vehicle that carries smaller space vehicles

orbit: the curved path of an object (such as a spaceship, satellite or moon) traveling fast enough that it does not fall to the surface of a more massive object (such as a planet) it is circling

planet: a ball-shaped body that circles around a star in a steady orbit

rocket: a tube-like device containing fuel that combusts (explodes) to move an object into space. It can also refer to a rocket engine. Multi-stage rockets are vehicles made of several rocket engines that are fired and discarded, one after another, at different stages during the flight.

satellite: a body that revolves around a planet. There are human-made satellites as well as natural satellites.

simulator: a machine that imitates certain conditions for the purpose of experimentation or training, such as training to go to space

solar system: the star system that is made up of the planets (including Earth), moons, comets, meteors, asteroids and other bodies that circle the Sun. (Our galaxy contains millions — possibly billions — of other star systems with planets and other bodies.)

solar wind: a stream of particles that "blow" out from the upper atmosphere of the Sun

space: the void between objects in the universe, also known as outer space. While Earth is technically in outer space, we often say that space begins 80–100 km (50–60 mi.) above the surface of Earth.

space agency: government organizations, such as the National Aeronautics and Space Administration (NASA), the Canadian Space Agency (CSA) and the European Space Agency (ESA), that have been established to explore the universe from Earth and in space

spaceship: a vehicle that can travel into and throughout space

space suit: a sealed suit that protects the wearer in space

space tourist: a person who vacations in space

space walk: any activity by an astronaut that takes place outside their ship while in space

suborbit: the path of an object (such as a spaceship) traveling fast enough to get into space but not to reach orbit

universe: everything in space. Our universe could be the entire cosmos, or there could be numerous universes that make up the cosmos.

SUBORBIT:
Surfboard Spaceships and
Giant-Panda

G-FORCES

▸ **Distance from Earth (average):** 80 to 160 km (50 to 100 mi.)
▸ **Total trip time:** 1 to 5 hours, including up to 4 minutes of weightlessness
▸ **When to go:** year-round (note: morning flights are less likely to be canceled due to high winds)

Highlights

▸ feel the thrill of a rocket-propelled launch

▸ experience the fun and sometimes scary effects of weightlessness

▸ take a picture or two of some out-of-this-world views

If you want to see some awesomely awe-inspiring views, including the blue haze of our atmosphere and the curve of our ball-shaped planet, a suborbital space adventure is for you. And luckily, getting into suborbital space (where a ship doesn't reach the speed or altitude needed to circle Earth) is the easiest part of space to get to. A number of companies are building rockets and planes to take you there. And some of these vehicles are already flying.

Before You Go

You'll have a few options when it comes to taking a trip into suborbit.

Scientists and engineers from the U.S.-based Blue Origin now have a version of their *New Shepard* capsule ready to carry six passengers from the high desert of West Texas into suborbit. In 2015, *New Shepard* became the world's first 100 percent reusable space rocket, taking off into suborbital space and then landing vertically on the same launch pad.

The WhiteKnightTwo (SpaceShipTwo's mother ship) in flight.

Blue Origin's New Shepard *rocket lifts off from its launch site in West Texas.*

In the same year Blue Origin sent a rocket to suborbit, Los Angeles–based space transportation company SpaceX reached orbit also using a 100 percent reusable rocket with a vertical takeoff and landing.

And in California's Mojave Desert a series of large hangars forms the flight-testing headquarters of Virgin Galactic and The Spaceship Company (the company that builds spacecraft for Virgin Galactic). There you'll find a school bus–sized rocket plane.

When you step into one of Virgin Galactic's sleek SpaceShipTwo rocket planes, you'll find a room that looks like a cross between a spaceship from a science-fiction movie and a fashion show runway. The walls are shiny white with neon blue lighting, and every seat has a view through several round windows. Up front, the cockpit has many large display screens, triangle-shaped windows looking out past the vehicle's nose, and a video-game-like flight stick for each of the two pilots.

To get into the air, SpaceShipTwo is carried under its mother ship, WhiteKnightTwo, which is a 43 m (141 ft.) wide carrier jet that has four engines and two fuselages (the main body of a plane that usually holds passengers or cargo). One of the fuselages is the main flight control center, while the other is an exact copy of a SpaceShipTwo interior, used for training future passengers.

World View is another company aiming to give you a taste of what it would be like to be in space. A capsule the size of a small room is lifted up 30 km (19 mi.) into "near space" using a giant balloon. It's not quite space, but from this altitude, passengers can look out to see the curve of Earth, look down on the clouds below and look up at the blackness of the cosmos above. The capsule uses a steerable, wing-shaped parachute to return to Earth. Unlike when using rockets or space planes, there are no g-forces to worry about during the roughly two-hour descent.

(Top left): The World View flight capsule travels above the clouds. (Top right): The capsule allows for 360-degree views through the viewports. (Bottom): The capsule, lifted by a giant balloon, floats high within the Earth's atmosphere. In between the two sits the steerable parachute.

We use composite structures like carbon and graphite, and even traditional materials like wood for some construction. We're basically making spaceships with surfboard technology.

— Peter Siebold, former SpaceShipTwo test pilot and director of flight operations for Virgin Galactic / The Spaceship Company

Your Flight

As a suborbital space adventurer, you might find yourself in the nose-cone capsule of Blue Origin's *New Shepard* rocket or in the futuristic-looking rocket of SpaceShipTwo.

When the stubby, 15 m (50 ft.) tall *New Shepard* launches, its engines fire for two minutes until the top of the rocket separates from the rest of the vehicle, taking you up into the cosmos.

Once your capsule reaches its highest point, you'll get to unbuckle your restraints to free-float during four minutes of weightlessness, all while looking out the largest windows ever put on a spaceship (more than 1m [3 ft.] tall).

When it's time to descend back to Earth, you'll strap yourself back into your seat. After several minutes of descent, parachutes open and you float the last few kilometers (or miles) down to the ground, coming to rest next to the rest of *New Shepard*, which has already landed nearby.

A flight on SpaceShipTwo involves a few more steps.

After taxiing down the runway, it's "liftoff!" as the WhiteKnightTwo mother ship spirals upward for over two hours, carrying SpaceShipTwo to an altitude of 15 km (9 mi.) above Earth.

At first, it'll feel a lot like an airplane ride. But once the mother ship reaches maximum altitude, hang on to your, well, pretty much everything! That's when you may hear the pilot saying, "3, 2, 1, release, release, release." At this point, you might want to remind yourself how much you like riding rollercoasters, as the rocket you are riding in is dropped from the mother ship — without its engines on.

Two seconds later, your pilot flips a switch to ignite the rocket's motor and you'll find your lungs, heart, liver and pretty much every other organ in your body pressed firmly against the back of your seat. Your pilot will then pull back on the flight stick to head straight up, taking you from zero to more than three times the speed of sound in just a few seconds!

During this one to two minutes of rocket-powered flight, you'll experience up to four times the normal gravity you feel on Earth. That means, if you weigh 30 to 40 kg (66 to 88 lb.), it would feel like having a giant panda lie on top of you. If you weigh more than 40 kg (88 lb.), add on a *baby* panda's worth of weight.

Whether you're on board *New Shepard* or SpaceShipTwo, once you near maximum altitude and your engines shut off, your arms and legs will start to feel lighter and the pressing feeling on your body will ease. You'll begin to breathe easy again.

Your freedom from gravity is about to begin!

For the next few minutes, your spaceship will take you to an approximate altitude of 80 km (50 mi.) above the surface of Earth, where you'll be high enough to see your home planet below and the blackness of the cosmos above.

> Flying SpaceShipTwo into space is like throwing a baseball straight up in the air. The second the rocket motor shuts off, it's like letting go of the baseball. Anyone inside that "baseball" starts to feel the effects of weightlessness at that point.
>
> — Peter Siebold, former SpaceShipTwo test pilot and director of flight operations for Virgin Galactic / The Spaceship Company

Things to Do

Now it's time to get the most out of your few minutes of microgravity. (In microgravity, you have the feeling of weightlessness, even though there is still a very small amount of gravity.)

Once that pesky 1g is no longer pressing down on you (as it has been your whole life), you might notice your hair or necklace start to float around you, or you might see your camera or phone floating in front of you. You'll find you've lost a little bit of your sense of smell. And if you're so moved by the view that you start to cry (lots of people do), your tears will pool in your eyes. You'll need to wipe and shake them away to be able to see clearly. (Your sweat will also cling to you!)

A view of a West Texas landscape and the curve of the Earth from Blue Origin's New Shepard rocket.

While you move around and explore the effects of weightlessness, you might even come up with a zero-gravity game to play with your fellow passengers. But you'll only have a few minutes, so make the most of it.

And definitely don't forget to take a look at that view!

- From here, you'll be able to see the layer of blue haze that makes up the Earth's atmosphere — the ocean of air that separates us from the rest of the universe.

- You'll also be able to see the surface of our planet in 3-D, as the land rises up off the water, and clouds float above everything.

- Try spotting stars out the windows. (They actually twinkle less up here because there's a lot less atmosphere to cause that twinkling we see on Earth.) Recognize any constellations?

- Make sure you take lots of pictures of the Earth and your view of space to share with friends and family. (Best profile picture ever!)

(Right): The sun glints off the Indian Ocean, as seen from the space shuttle Discovery.
(Below): Earth as seen from the Crew Capsule of Blue Origin's New Shepard *rocket.*

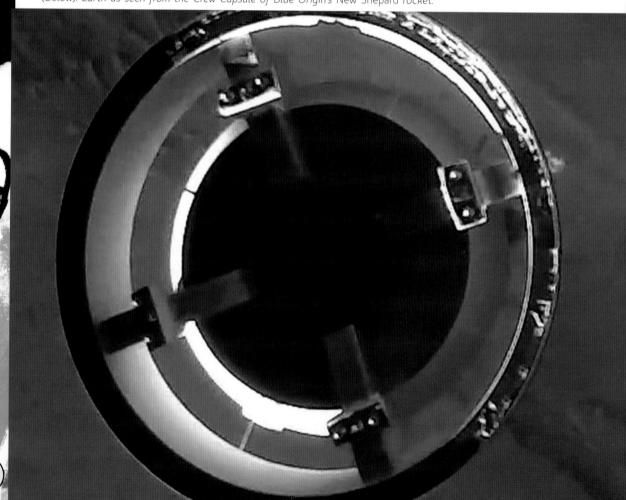

On the way back down from your suborbital flight, buckle up for the thirty seconds to one minute of consciousness-losing, barf-inducing g-forces (4 to 6 gs!) that you'll experience while your ship quickly slows down through the thickening atmosphere before landing. (Here's one way to imagine experiencing high g-forces: if you weigh 30 to 40 kg [66 to 88 lb.], 6 gs would feel like someone parked a large motorcycle on your chest.)

After getting through those maximum g-forces, you'll have a few dozen more minutes to catch your breath during your ship's final glide or parachute back down to solid ground.

The Tower of Terror in Johannesburg, South Africa, is the only amusement ride in the world where you experience 6 gs — but only for two seconds of the ride.

When I went up on a zero-gravity [airplane] flight for training, being weightless felt like swimming, just without the pressure of water on your skin. A guy about my size and I started tossing this girl about half our size back and forth while she was curled up into a ball. (It was her idea.)

— Scotty Eastbourn,
Propulsion Design Engineer,
Virgin Galactic

Space Tour Insider

- SpaceShipTwo doesn't have a front landing wheel. Instead, it uses a ski made of wood that pops out the bottom of its nose and scrapes along the ground when it touches down.

- After its final test flights, SpaceShipTwo's prototype (the original model) — SpaceShipOne — was placed in the Smithsonian Institution's National Air and Space Museum. It hangs next to Bell X-1 (the first aircraft to go faster than the speed of sound) and the *Spirit of St Louis* (the first plane to fly non-stop across the Atlantic Ocean).

- In 2015, Blue Origin's *New Shepard* became the first rocket in history to make both a controlled vertical takeoff and a controlled vertical landing from space. The entire *New Shepard* rocket can be re-used again and again. Before this, rockets took off and then parachuted back to Earth unpowered, and only part of the rocket could be re-used.

- The balloon that will carry World View travelers to near-space will be 1.1 million cubic meters (40 million cubic feet) in size.

- Among the first to buy tickets to suborbital space were actors Tom Hanks and Brad Pitt, recording artists Justin Bieber and Katy Perry, as well as world-famous scientist Stephen Hawking.

- The youngest passenger to buy a ticket to fly in suborbital space is from Calgary, Alberta. He was 16 years old when he bought his ticket for a trip on SpaceShipTwo.

(Left): A view of the Red Sea as seen from the International Space Station.
(Below): Scientist Stephen Hawking floats in weightlessness aboard a zero-gravity "vomit comet" flight.

EARTH ORBIT:
Around the World in
90 MINUTES

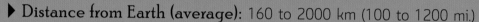

▶ **Distance from Earth (average):** 160 to 2000 km (100 to 1200 mi.)
▶ **Total trip time:** up to a week, including 8 minutes of rocket-powered flight to reach orbit and 90 minutes per complete Earth orbit
▶ **When to go:** year-round

Highlights

▶ see the wonders of Earth from hundreds of kilometers (or miles) above

▶ watch the Sun rise and set on our planet, over and over and over

▶ witness the colorful dance of the aurora from high above

▶ find out what life is like on the International Space Station (ISS)

▶ experience daily life in weightlessness

Life in orbit is possibly one of the greatest adventures experienced by humans so far. Orbiting the Earth on the International Space Station (ISS), you can look down to see whole countries at once, and spot some spectacular features on the surface, such as the Caribbean Sea, islands scattered throughout the oceans and the coral shelves off Australia's Great Barrier Reef. Then when the Sun sets, plunging you into darkness, you'll be able to see lights from cities, highways and industrial areas, such as oil fields. And just in case you missed anything the first time around, you'll have the chance to see it all again every 90 minutes, the time it takes to complete one orbit of your home planet Earth.

Before You Go

Think of an orbit as an enormous game of space tug-of-war in which a smaller object (your spaceship or a space station) falls away from a massive object (a planet or moon) until the larger object's gravity tugs it back, causing the smaller object to swing around and around, in a stretched-out ellipse. As long as your spaceship isn't going fast enough to break free of this gravitational tug or slow enough that it crashes down onto the object you're orbiting, you'll keep orbiting forever.

The Florida peninsula as seen from the space shuttle Discovery.

Your Flight

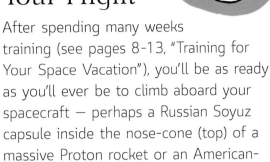

After spending many weeks training (see pages 8-13, "Training for Your Space Vacation"), you'll be as ready as you'll ever be to climb aboard your spacecraft — perhaps a Russian Soyuz capsule inside the nose-cone (top) of a massive Proton rocket or an American-made Dragon capsule sitting atop one of SpaceX's Falcon boosters.

Once safely strapped in on the Soyuz (which Dennis Tito and other early space tourists traveled in), you'll hear the ignition of the central core engines followed by the crack-and-boom of the booster engines. With a chest-rattling roar, you lift off and quickly soar into the air. It'll take

If you're flying in SpaceX's roomy, seven-seat Dragon 2 capsule, your launch will begin with the firing of your ship's main engines (at about 10 percent more thrust than the old space shuttles) and a quick acceleration up and away from the Earth. As gravity pushes you back into your carbon-fiber seat, you can watch large touch-screens to monitor your spacecraft's status and launch progress. Dragon 2 can fly itself, or be controlled by the crew onboard or mission-control back down on Earth.

you a little extra effort to breathe with the extreme g-forces acting against your body. Your heart rate will also increase and it may feel like the skin on your face is being stretched back.

Fortunately, these intense sensations stop two minutes or so after launch when the booster engines fall away from your ship. Three minutes later, the core engines shut off and fall away. After five minutes, the smaller upper stage finally shuts off, and you and your van-sized capsule continue to drift upward into orbit.

Over the next six hours, your capsule — going a speed 23 times the speed of sound — catches up to the ISS. To dock, your spacecraft carefully moves up to a docking port at the ISS until they touch. After both are pressurized, the two crafts are clamped together using adapters and the doorways between the two open.

Once docked at history's largest space outpost, you'll be welcomed to the 100 m (350 ft.) wide station by professional astronauts from different countries who work on science experiments and perform the daily operations of the ISS. The ISS usually has six full-time crew members, but for short periods of time there might be a few others who are either visiting or getting ready to take over for other crew members.

As a space tourist, you may decide to help with some of the work being done on board (if you're allowed) or even run some of your own experiments. Or you could choose to just enjoy a once-in-a-lifetime vacation.

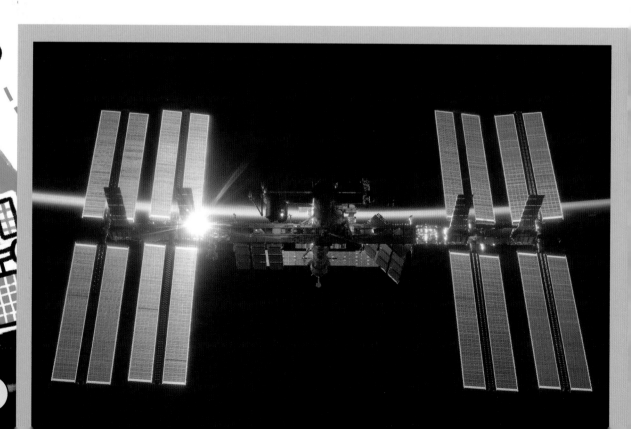

The six days I spent on the space station were the happiest of my life. Because I wasn't being paid to work up there, I could spend the entire time there enjoying the view and the rest of the experience. From watching the different textures of land and water glide by below me, to flying through the air like a superhero — it's something I hope we all have the chance to do at some point in our lives.

— Dennis Tito, the world's first space tourist

The International Space Station orbits about 400 km (250 mi.) above the surface of our planet. At this altitude, you're traveling 28 000 km/h (17 000 m.p.h.), circling the Earth about once every 90 minutes.

(Left): The ISS, along with the thin line of Earth's atmosphere, is seen from the space shuttle Discovery as it undocks from the station in March 2009.

Thirty-one astronauts and 144 non-astronauts have died in accidents related to spaceflight so far. This includes three Spaceship Company staff killed in 2007 by an explosion during an on-the-ground test for one of their rocket engines. Then in 2014, test co-pilot Michael Alsbury died after the wings of the air-braking descent system of VSS *Enterprise* (Virgin Galactic's first SpaceShipTwo) were deployed (set off) too early during the flight up through the atmosphere. Pilot Peter Siebold, however, ejected and parachuted to safety, escaping with serious injuries.

When You Get There

In many ways, living on the ISS is just like living in a house on Earth … if that house was one you could never leave, traveled at 28 000 km/h (17 000 m.p.h.), made its own air and water, and had the best view in the universe.

Of course, there's the small matter of living in almost no gravity, which makes everything from eating to going to the bathroom feel like an Olympic feat. Even taking a deep breath can only happen thanks to some of the most advanced technology ever invented.

In order to keep a steady supply of air for you to breathe, the ISS uses two systems: one pulls oxygen out of the wastewater from bathing and going to the bathroom, while another removes the toxic carbon dioxide being exhaled by everyone onboard, as well as any methane (from farts) and ammonia (from sweat).

And because only a limited amount of water can be transported to and stored aboard the ISS, almost all (93 percent) of what's brought up is recycled. For bathroom visits and bathing, you use vacuum-like hoses to remove liquid to be recycled for other uses. Sweat, urine and wastewater are filtered and reused creating roughly 6000 L (1600 gal.) of water that can be used on the ISS each year.

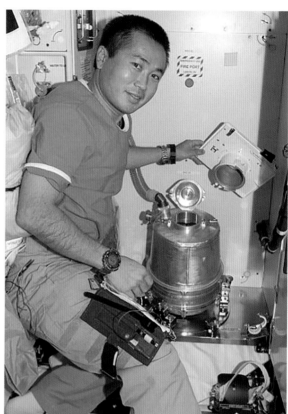

(Top): A waste and hygiene compartment on the ISS
(Middle): Astronaut Koichi Wakata performs the daily flush of the potable water dispenser on the ISS.
(Bottom): A water bubble is squeezed out of astronaut Naoko Yamazaki's beverage container.

At mealtimes in orbit, you can get nearly any type of food you want ... with some slight modifications. For example, you can have your favorite peanut butter and jelly sandwich — as long as it's made with a flatbread like a tortilla. You can't use sliced bread in case the floating crumbs clog instruments. They can even pose a health risk if they get in your eyes or if you inhale them.

The rest of the menu can include a whole variety of main courses, vegetables, pasta side dishes, sandwiches, fruit, snacks, desserts and breakfast treats, as well as condiments and sauces, all available packaged in vacuum-sealed pouches that keep the food fresh. (For some meals you'll need to add water to foods that have been sent to the space station dehydrated, or had their moisture removed.)

And when you're thirsty? Mix some dried crystals and water to make juices, tea, coffee and other drinks.

And all of these dining experiences can be enjoyed at a table next to the most exclusive view in the solar system (even though you won't actually need the table).

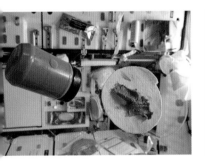

A floating snack of peanut butter and tortilla on the space shuttle Discovery.

Astronaut Luca Parmitano gathers his floating food packages on the ISS.

Astronauts Peggy Whitson (left) and Valery Korzun (right) eat floating hamburgers on the ISS.

In 2015, astronauts on the ISS successfully grew their own lettuce in order to enjoy some fresh produce as part of their meals.

Things to Do

While on the ISS, you'll likely spend a lot of your time looking out the 3 m (9 ft.) wide, dome-like Cupola module — which has the largest set of windows ever put into space.

Looking out the windows of the ISS's Cupola observation module you can see huge objects on the Earth's surface, such as large cities or even a 20 000 hectare (50 000 acre) collection of greenhouses on the southern tip of Spain. To see smaller objects, such as airports, dams, monuments or large ships at sea, though, you'll just need to use binoculars or a camera with a zoom lens.

From orbit, you can see the stunning dance of the aurora back on Earth: country-sized curtains of colorful light that flicker and wave in the skies, thanks to outbursts of energy from the Sun.

Imagine gazing down into the eye of a hurricane from 400 km (250 mi.) up. Or seeing a sunrise light up entire countries. In the 90 minutes it takes the ISS to circle the Earth, you'll get an astronaut's view of many famous landmarks around the world, possibly including:

▸ Australia's Great Barrier Reef
▸ the Grand Canyon
▸ Walt Disney World Resort (using a zoom lens, you can even see individual parks like Epcot and the Magic Kingdom)
▸ London, Paris, New York, Toronto and other large cities (especially when they're lit up at night)
▸ Dubai's human-made island neighborhoods, Palm Islands and The World Islands
▸ the Great Pyramids in Egypt

(Left): Dubai
(Middle): Almeria, Spain
(Right): Steam plume from the active volcano Mount Gharat on the island of Gaua.

While some space tourists (sometimes called "spaceflight participants" when they conduct science experiments and do other things besides just vacationing) do serious work in space, career astronauts actually get to do some pretty fun things when they're not on the job. In 2013, while in orbit, Canadian astronaut Commander Chris Hadfield sang and played guitar while collaborating with numerous musicians back on Earth to record the album *Space Sessions: Songs from a Tin Can.*

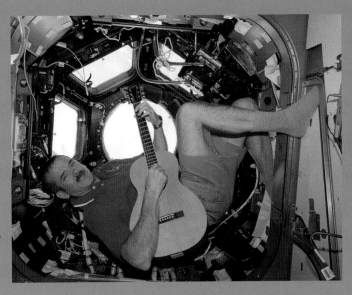

Other orbital pastimes might include perfecting your superhero-style flying. By pushing off from one end of the ISS's modules, you can try floating all the way to the other end — about 30 m (100 ft.) away. Or maybe you'll be so inspired by your experience, you'll want to do something creative: Iranian American businesswoman Anousheh Ansari became the first person to write a blog in space when she was in orbit.

From flying like a superhero to touring the world in 90 minutes, a vacation in orbit will change the way you see your home planet forever.

(Top): Astronaut Chris Hadfield plays his guitar in the Cupola of the ISS.

(Bottom): Spaceflight participant Anousheh Ansari shows off a plant that was grown on the ISS.

Suni Williams's Top Five Things to See in Earth Orbit

During her two missions to the ISS, NASA astronaut Suni Williams made seven space walks and spent more time in orbit than any other woman in history (a combined total of nearly a year). In her own words, here are Suni's five favorite things to see on Earth from orbit:

▶ **The Grand Canyon, Arizona, United States**: "The Grand Canyon is impressive! You can see so many colors (earth tones, oranges, pinks). From orbit (through a camera zoom lens) you can even see the green of the river that runs through the bottom of the canyon."

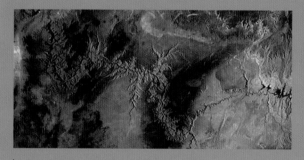

▶ **Natural wonders**: "Some of the things that make you feel like the planet is alive, like cloud formations and lightning from above ... You can see a lightning strike in Texas and another one where it's 'equalizing' [balancing out the electrical charge in the region] across the border in Canada."

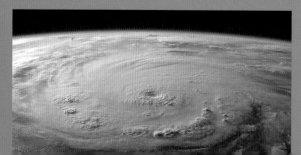

▶ **The Himalayas, Asia**: "You can look down on some of the world's highest peaks (including Mount Everest) and see the concept of plate tectonics in action."

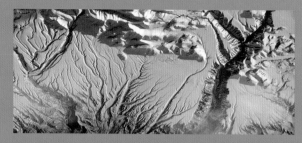

▶ **The Caribbean Sea**: "You can see right into the water ... The colors of the ocean are always changing and you can see the currents from the sand and reefs. Any time I had a bad day, I looked down at the Caribbean."

▶ **Human-made wonders**: "While I couldn't see the Great Wall of China (some astronauts have been able to see it through a camera lens), I could see the pyramids in Egypt and the Statue of Liberty in New York City (using a powerful camera lens) because of the angles of the Sun and the shadows they cast."

Space Tour Insider

- Although the inside of the ISS has about the same amount of space as a Boeing 747 passenger jet, the outside is much bigger — about the size of a football field or five NHL hockey rinks.

- Cell phones work just fine on the ISS. Email, though, arrives only two to three times per day.

- In 2009, after wearing a circus clown nose for the pre-flight photos before his trip to the ISS, Canadian Cirque du Soleil co-founder Guy Laliberté took part in a two-hour, multi-city show while in orbit to help raise awareness of global drinking-water problems.

- Residents of the ISS have access to what amounts to a full gym, with everything from a stationary bike (which they strap themselves onto) to a resistance machine that recreates the challenge of weight lifting. People who spend more than a week or so in orbit need to work out for hours each day to help prevent the bone-density loss that happens when your body isn't working against any gravity.

- While Dennis Tito's flight cost him U.S. $20 million, he hopes orbital space trips could someday go for under $1 million. (Suborbital trips are already much less.)

- Microsoft executive Charles Simonyi should start collecting frequent-flyer miles for trips into space. To date, he is the only tourist to travel into the cosmos twice.

- While in orbit, people on the ISS have done everything from running the Boston Marathon (using a treadmill to run the equivalent distance runners traveled on Earth) to participating in stunts where people on Earth successfully "waved" at those living on the station using lasers and an airport-style searchlight.

Equipped with a bungee harness, astronaut Sunita (Suni) Williams exercises on the treadmill, called the TVIS, on the ISS.

ORBITAL CRUISE:

All Aboard Your

SPACE YACHT

- ▶ **Distance from Earth (average):** 1000 to 500 000 km (600 to 310 000 mi.)
- ▶ **Total trip time:** 1 to 2 weeks
- ▶ **When to go:** year-round, beginning approximately 2030

Highlights

- ▶ dock at exciting ports in high-Earth orbit and beyond
- ▶ chow down at a floating buffet
- ▶ swim in a zero-gravity pool

On Earth, lots of people go on ocean cruises, but how would you like to take a cruise to an out-of-this-world destination? Instead of a tropical paradise, how about a trip out into the amazing wonders of the universe?

Before You Go

Engineers, pilots and space architects are working toward building spaceships to take passengers on orbital cruises. Similar to the way an ocean-going cruise ship leaves a main port to visit different places along its route, people would board a space cruise ship at its home port in low Earth orbit to depart for a cruise to high Earth orbit.

Engineers working on designs for space cruise ships have learned a lot from the experiences of astronauts and from the development of newer technologies such as next-generation g-suits, solid rocket fuel (rather than liquid) and multi-stage rockets (which are made of several rocket engines that are fired and then dropped, one after another, at different stages).

Space architects like John Spencer, the president of the Space Tourism Society, are trying to make space travel both fun and glamorous — unlike early (probably stinky) space missions that had astronauts traveling in what must have felt like a tin can, without luxuries such as flush toilets, running tap water, showers or even deodorant.

The design elements of orbital cruise ships will likely be both practical and decorative. For example, a ship's cool-looking fins and sweeping wings might also function as energy-collecting solar panels. (After all, if you're paying big bucks for the vacation of a lifetime, you want your ride to look good.)

But there are still some challenges to overcome before these ships become a reality.

For instance, huge space cruise ships and orbital yachts would have to be taken up to orbit in pieces, similar to the way the International Space Station was constructed. That's because there's currently no rocket large enough to transport such enormous ships into space all in one piece. Their huge size also means they would only be able to exist in zero gravity and could never land on Earth or anywhere else with gravity.

One option is assembling large inflatable modules (or rooms). The deflated modules would be folded to fit inside rockets and then sent up into orbit. There, they'd be inflated and connected to other modules to make one big ship.

John Spencer believes these high-tech fabric modules would be more durable than rigid metal modules, particularly when it comes to the impact of small pieces of space debris. Inflatable modules might also be able to do cool things like change color or even become transparent to make star-gazing even easier.

Space cruise ships will also need to be equipped with the most cutting-edge technology, such as air circulation and recycling systems and plumbing that would run on rechargeable solar batteries. This way, there'd be no need for complicated wiring, making assembling and running a modular ship much simpler. High-efficiency batteries are already being used in the aerospace industry for things like cabin pressure, brakes and some of the flaps that control direction in Boeing's 787 Dreamliner.

Astronaut Kate Rubins inside the experimental Bigelow Expandable Activity Module (BEAM).

Space architect John Spencer has what might be the coolest non-astronaut space job in the world. For more than a decade, he has designed concepts for future large-scale space tourism vehicles and attractions. His designs for spaceships, habitats and Earth-based space tourism attractions have appeared in numerous articles and TV shows. He also created the first interior designs for NASA's SPACEHAB science lab module, which flew on the space shuttles over a dozen times. But perhaps his coolest creation is a concept for what he calls an "orbital super-yacht": *Destiny* is a luxury craft made of inflatable modules and wing-like solar panels that make it look like a beautiful exotic fish.

> For years, I've thought of space tourism as a lot like being on a cruise ship: you're on a fantastic journey on a vehicle that stops at different ports of call, but you also have all sorts of activities to do on board as you travel.
>
> — *John Spencer, former NASA engineer, president of the Space Tourism Society*

Artist Jeff Coatney's depiction of John Spencer's orbital space yacht Destiny.

Your Flight

The first part of your space cruise will likely begin with you leaving Earth in a smaller rocket or space plane, similar to one used on suborbital adventures. This will be your "shuttle," taking you to the main cruise spacecraft, which will probably be docked in low Earth orbit.

On a larger cruise ship, there may be cabins for you and your fellow passengers to sleep in. On smaller ships, there may just be places on the walls for you to strap yourself and your bedding to. Don't want to be strapped to the wall when there's all that space where you can lounge around? Catch a mid-air snooze floating in microgravity — but you just might get a rude awakening when you drift into a wall. (Actually, many astronauts say they had the best sleeps of their lives while in space.)

Just like on a traditional cruise ship, there will be staff to assist you. But on a space cruise, this will be a person trained in zero-g hospitality or it might even be a floating robot "concierge" that makes sure you've got everything you need to enjoy your cruise. According to John Spencer, these robots could be programmed to provide individual climate control by blowing hotter or cooler air in your direction as they float near you (something early astronauts in those sweaty, overheated capsules would have probably appreciated).

And what's a cruise without opportunities for taking in the sights? Like Spencer's design for the orbital yacht *Destiny*, space cruise ships could be equipped with observation areas for taking in the most out-of-this-world views. Future space cruises will mean "sailing" away from Earth for a set of spectacular sights.

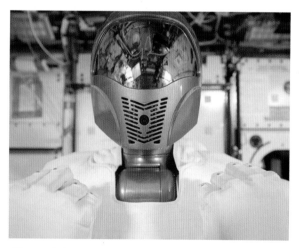

(Above): Robonaut 2 (R2), the humanoid robot astronaut helper, on the ISS.

(Right): An artist's view of the Earth eclipsing the Sun from the perspective of the Moon.

- Future space cruise ships could fly far enough so you can see the glowing orange ring of light around the Earth during a lunar eclipse.

- You might have a front-row view of a comet or asteroid passing by, close enough that you can see its craters, crevices, flat plains and more.

- You could fly over Tycho, the most spectacular crater on the Moon, for an up-close look at its 1500 km (1000 mi.) long rays. (These lines look something like the spokes of a wheel and were probably caused by the impact of a comet or asteroid long ago.)

- You may travel to the Moon's "far side" (from Earth) to see the mountains, ridges and craters impossible to see from our home planet and maybe even watch the Earth rise over the lunar horizon.

You really have to build up the muscles in your tummy to do a "number two" in space ... When you go into the bathroom the first few times, you have to concentrate A LOT ...

— Suni Williams, ISS crew member and NASA astronaut

Someday, there might be a space resort to dock at, where passengers can leave their ship and enjoy everything from playing sports to eating, all in zero-g. But while all that weightlessness might be fun for a while, you'll probably want a break at some point.

Space resorts could be equipped with artificial gravity created using technology similar to g-force centrifuge simulators on Earth. In other words, the resort (or just a section of it) would be designed as a giant spinning wheel, creating a comfortable 1 g force inside. While that might sound like science fiction, scientists have been thinking about this concept for more than a century. In fact, in 2011, NASA even looked into adding a rotating wheel module to the ISS.

Things to Do

Wet & Wild in Zero~G

Cruise ships usually have pools, but how would that work in zero gravity?

On Earth, droplets of water can only get so big before the surface tension (the way water molecules hold tightly together to form droplets) breaks and the drops spill over. But in space, surface tension wins out over gravity so that blob of water stays more or less ball-shaped, like one giant droplet.

On large space cruise ships, the "swimming pool" might be a huge blob of water in an enclosed room. To swim, you could push off from the walls and "dive" into the water. Even if this caused the sphere of water to break apart, blowing fans and the walls in the room could help contain the water so it eventually collects back together. And of course when swimming in zero gravity, you wouldn't drop to the bottom or float to the top like you do on Earth.

Smaller space yachts may have zero-gravity hot tubs instead of full-size pools: John Spencer designed something he calls the "hot sphere" — a five- to six-person-sized ball of water that has been first heated by lasers. Here again, the surface tension of water holds it together in a ball.

Tastes Like Space ...

On a long-haul, multi-month trip in space, the food would be similar to what astronauts eat today: vacuum-sealed fruits and vegetables, sterilized breads (tortillas, for example) and pre-cooked meats — food that keeps for months and doesn't spoil. Not very exciting.

But on a one- to two-week space cruise, you could have almost any food you'd eat on Earth, as long as it could be eaten safely and without mess in zero-g. (Actually, why worry about the mess? You're on vacation!)

On a space cruise ship, restaurants and food courts would need to be built to work in weightlessness. What could this mean? Maybe the utensils would be Velcro-ed to your table, and drink dispensers could work like a fuel pump by squirting liquid directly into sealed bottles. And the food displays at the buffet could be gravity-defying arrangements impossible on Earth.

So, how about a slice of mid-air veggie pizza or a hot dog washed down with a high-speed blast of chocolate milk?

- With melted cheese holding all the toppings in place, pizza is a good space food option — as long as the crust is made from dough that isn't crumbly. (Remember, crumbs can float around, getting into your eyes, nose and throat, not to mention the space cruise ship's ventilation systems.)

- As long as you hold on to it tightly, a hot dog topped with ketchup, mustard, relish and other condiments would do just fine in weightlessness. In fact, lots of sauces make their way into space in fast-food-style packets. NASA even sends cranberry sauce into orbit in the same single-serving packages it comes in at restaurants and cafeterias. (Just be sure to hold the packets close to what you're squeezing them onto.)

- You can also slurp some chocolate milk out of a sealed container. (Back to sippy cups for you!)

What's more, in weightlessness, you could make the world's tallest sundae or ice-cream cone — with no worries about dropping a scoop on the floor. Or what about playing Frisbee with your breakfast waffles? (To prevent things from getting messy — and dangerous — these cones and waffles would be specially made to be soft.) And instead of pouring your syrup onto your waffle, you could squirt syrup into the air and throw your waffle into its path. In zero gravity, it's more about *fun* dining than fine dining!

Since it's harder to taste in zero gravity, you might want to try ordering some of these flavorful dishes already taste-tested on NASA and ISS missions:

- tacos with salsa and hot sauce

- a shrimp cocktail with spicy mayonnaise-and-tomato dip

- Creole jambalaya

- dried fruit desserts (for the concentrated fruit flavor)

- pasta with cream or tomato sauce with two to three times the spice you'd normally have

- sour lemonade

When you first get to space, you won't have much of an appetite. You're actually not really hungry for the first few days because food isn't weighing down on your stomach. Plus, everything's so exciting you might forget to eat for a while.

— Suni Williams

A Night Out in the Movie Sphere

Your first day or two on your cruise might be pretty hard on your body as it gets used to such a weird new environment. So at some point, you're probably just going to want to kick back and relax ... maybe by watching a movie.

In the weightlessness of an orbital cruise ship, this might mean taking in a flick while floating around inside a ball-shaped theater where the walls themselves serve as the screen. In other words, you'd get to experience "surround screen" rather than just surround sound.

Or new technology might allow people to float around freely and interact with all parts of an interactive screen. These might also be developed as virtual-reality environments in 3-D, giving you the feeling that you're floating around places you couldn't otherwise, such as through clouds or the deepest parts of the ocean.

Space Tour Insider

- Plans for John Spencer's orbital space yacht *Destiny* and other larger space cruise ships include a huge 20 m (60 ft.) diameter room called the "float sphere." Although the whole vessel would be without gravity, this open area would be large enough for vacationers to spin, fly and somersault through the air to their hearts' content.

- American hotel chain owner Robert Bigelow had a one-third-scale, working inflatable space habitat placed into orbit in 2006. A full-sized version could someday be the first spacecraft used as a full-time orbital hotel.

- Pop beverages can actually be dangerous in the final frontier. Carbonated drinks can cause problems when the carbon dioxide bubbles remain in your digestive system instead of burped out. (You can't belch in space — you'd vomit instead!)

- Space agencies have developed a special "barf bag" for the final frontier: it has a sealable opening to make sure bits of your orbital upchuck don't float away, and a napkin-like liner you can use to wipe your mouth.

- Want a cool job? Space tourism isn't just about the tourists: soon the space vacation industry will need to employ people in hospitality, navigation, entertainment, engineering and computer science. There will probably even need to be a space version of the coast guard to enforce space tourism bylaws and carry out any emergency rescue operations.

The MOON:
Crater Skiing and
BAMBOO HOTELS

■ ■

▶ **Distance from Earth (average):** 385 000 km (239 000 mi.)
▶ **Total trip time:** 6 days travel time, plus time spent on the Moon
▶ **When to go:** year-round, beginning approximately 2025

Highlights

▶ try low-gravity sports

▶ watch the "phases" of the Earth from the Moon

▶ race a moon buggy around the edge of a crater

Thinking about a vacation on the Moon? Whether you're looking forward to skiing down the dusty slopes of a lunar crater or watching your home planet rise slowly over the horizon, remember to change your social media status to "Traveling to a whole other world today."

Before You Go

The Moon orbits Earth every 27.3 days and is its only natural satellite. It's much smaller than Earth — 50 Moons could fit inside our planet! And unlike our home planet, the Moon has almost no atmosphere to protect it from meteors — it's these collisions that give the Moon its famous craters. That lack of atmosphere also means the Moon has boiling hot temperatures during the day and crushing cold at night.

In 1969, NASA's Apollo 11 mission landed on the Moon, and Neil Armstrong became the first of only 12 humans to step on the rocky lunar surface. So far anyway. Although no other human has made that visit since 1972, there's lots of interest in returning. Evidence of water on the Moon's surface has scientists wondering if the Moon could one day be used as a base for ships taking off to the outer planets.

(Above): Astronaut Buzz Aldrin's bootprint on the Moon, from the Apollo 11 mission. Along with Neil Armstrong, he took one of the first steps on the Moon, on July 20, 1969.

(Left): Apollo 11 lifts off for the Moon on July 16, 1969.

Your Flight

In the 1960s and 1970s, it took power equal to a small atomic bomb for NASA's huge Saturn rockets to carry astronauts and gear to the Moon. And even with modern advancements in rocket efficiency, breaking free of Earth's gravity to travel to another world is still thunderously intense.

Imagine this: With a blinding flash, massive engines fire and flames roll out from under your rocket ship, which starts to rise into the air. Seconds later, the deafening *boom* reaches spectators a dozen kilometers (or miles) away and the feeling of a shockwave smacks deep into their chests as the ground shakes. The multi-stage craft roars into space, like a giant train to the stars.

As your Moon rocket begins to pick up speed, you'll experience up to 4 gs of force: every vein in your body feels like it's about to explode, the skin on your cheeks feels like its being pulled up to your hairline, and you start to have trouble lifting your hands and arms.

After several minutes of high-speed accelerating, a powerful jolt rocks you as the main engines cut out and the lower section of your rocket detaches to fall back to Earth. Finally you stop feeling like a sheet of plywood is on top of your chest and someone is riding a bike back and forth across it. Phew! You can breathe easy again.

You'll spend the next few days — the time it will take to reach the Moon — gently coasting. For now, life in your capsule will be pretty cramped, but at least you'll have lots of time to enjoy the view as your ship coasts into orbit about 80 km (50 mi.) above the lunar surface.

Landing on the Moon is *a lot* easier than landing on Earth. (Returning to Earth, a spacecraft is pulled downward by the planet's gravity for a crushing, fiery re-entry through the atmosphere. But you don't need to worry about that *now*.) Because of the Moon's lower gravity and almost non-existent atmosphere, a quick blast from a lander's maneuvering jets (think mini rockets) is all that's needed to nudge your craft gently down to the lunar surface.

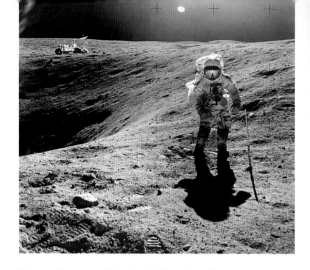

(Above): Astronaut Charles M. Duke Jr. collects lunar samples near the rim of Plum Crater. A parked lunar rover can be seen in the background.

(Below): This panoramic view shows the first time a Lunar Roving Vehicle was deployed on the Moon, in 1971, by Apollo 15 astronauts Dave Scott (pictured) and Jim Irwin.

Next Stop, the Moon

Several companies — some that employ former NASA staff — claim they can build a ship to fly you to the Moon as soon as you want construction to begin. The catch? They'll need U.S. $100 million per person to fly you around the Moon (or U.S. $750 million per person if you want to land and walk on it).

While none of those missions have lifted off, in 2017, SpaceX announced it had taken a deposit from two people who would be the first paying customers for the company to fly to the Moon.

When You Get There

An airless wasteland with a temperature that ranges between 120°C (250°F) during sunlit hours to -150°C (-240°F) at night, the lunar landscape isn't the most inviting environment. But equipped with a modern space suit, you'll be able to walk around on the Moon's surface comfortably for hours.

Due to the Moon's lower mass, its gravity is only one-sixth that of Earth's. But that doesn't mean moving around is always easier. You would be able to jump much

higher than on Earth, *but* it would also take you longer to land. And walking would take more time since your feet would be slower to reach the ground as you step.

Also, navigation can be tricky because of the Moon's almost total lack of atmosphere and landscape that doesn't change much over short distances. What looks like a small dip in the ground might actually be a steep crater ... and the lower gravity isn't enough to cushion a 100 m (300 ft.) fall.

You'll also need to watch out for the fine dust called *regolith* that makes up much of the lunar surface. With almost no moisture and little gravity to weigh it down, this fine powder gets into *everything*: the seals on space suits, moving parts on lunar rovers, personal electronics and more. Regolith might be just an annoyance at first, but over time it can wear down joints and fasteners on equipment and even pose a threat to your lungs when breathed in if brought indoors on clothing.

Of course, before anyone can truly vacation in the hostile environment of the Moon, we'll need new ways of thinking about tools, transportation and architecture. Extreme temperatures and solar radiation mean having the right buildings to call home is a high priority. A number of space agencies and companies are looking at ways to build temporary base camps and even hotels.

When designing life-supporting structures on the Moon, lunar architects may consider these approaches:

1) Bring materials from Earth, such as the rigid metal containers that were used for the ISS. Another option might be easy-to-pack inflatable modules (rooms). U.S.-based Bigelow Aerospace has already developed several types of inflatable habitats that could be used on the Moon.

2) Use materials found on the lunar surface, such as rock and sand. One recent NASA study even suggested using microwaves to melt lunar dirt to make a smooth, cement-like material for paving roads, constructing buildings and more. A European Space Agency study suggested the possibility of using 3-D printers to make bricks and other building blocks out of lunar surface.

3) Grow building materials on the Moon. Some space engineers have proposed that seeds of bamboo plants (sometimes used as building material on Earth) could be sent to the Moon, where a large supply of the strong, resilient wood could be grown in enclosed domes. Between the Moon's low gravity, ample sunlight (no clouds!) and water brought from Earth (or maybe melted from the ice found in some lunar craters), it may be possible for these sturdy plants to be used to build structures.

(Above): A NASA concept of a plant growth module.

(Left): An artist's rendering of doing construction work on a lunar base.

Of course, all buildings would need to be equipped with built-in life support, heating, sewage and communication systems. They'd also need to be equipped with furniture and appliances that work in the Moon's low-gravity environment. For example, beds might require padded "walls" around the edges to keep you from bouncing off and onto the floor as you toss and turn — kind of like a crib for grown-ups.

Things to Do

Once you've mastered the basic challenges of living on the Moon, there'll be lots of opportunities for space adventuring across the lunar landscape.

"Earthrise" over the lunar horizon, as viewed from the Lunar Reconnaissance Orbiter.

Earth-Gazing and Other Sightseeing

Most of us think nothing of being able to look up and see the Moon, glowing in Earth's night sky. But imagine how cool it would be to look out into the dark sky and see Earth — a huge, blue-green-white ball, slowly turning as it hangs in the sky. It would look four times wider and more than a dozen times bigger in the sky than the Moon looks from our home planet. (Although because the Moon is gravitationally locked so that the same side is always facing Earth, you could never have a view of Earth from the so-called far side of the Moon.) And depending on when you visit, the Moon's sky may be dark enough to see *tens of thousands* of stars — far more than are visible from Earth at night.

While you're touring the Moon's surface, you might also want to look for some of the human-made creations there, such as the lower section of NASA's Apollo 11 lunar lander still on the surface from the 1969 landing or the reflectors that scientists beam lasers at when measuring the distance to the Moon. You might also be able to check out sites for future lunar-mining operations or a super powerful space observatory.

Low-Gravity Sports

The first game of golf has already been played on the Moon — sort of. In 1971, NASA astronaut Alan Shepard hit two golf balls across the Fra Mauro Highlands (the part of the Moon where Apollo 14 had landed). He joked that the balls went for "miles and miles and miles." (It was actually just a few hundred meters [or yards], which is not bad considering Shepard was wearing a bulky space suit and hit the balls with a golf club head strapped to the arm of a tool for gathering soil samples.)

There are all sorts of possibilities for sports on the Moon. In low-gravity, imagine what your jumping ability could mean for gymnastics or off-road biking. You'd never be in danger of flying off the surface, but the results of even the smallest jump here would be a spectacular achievement on Earth.

What will the low gravity mean for a ball game? In an LBA (that would be the Lunar Basketball Association) game, you'd be able to jump six times higher than you could on Earth. So instead of playing with nets that are 3 m (10 ft.) off the ground, your nets could be 18 m (60 ft.) off the ground. (Although since your eyesight and aim would be no better, maybe half that net height would be more fair.) And for a game of volleyball, the nets would need to be the size of passenger jets to keep the same dimensions and still be high enough for a challenge.

Some other exciting possibilities for Moon sports are skiing and snowboarding. While it's not easy to downhill ski in dirt on Earth, smooth lunar regolith and the lack of gravity would mean that you could shred some serious soil. And since we know that the ground at most of the sites the Apollo astronauts visited is uneven, there would be lots of moguls nearby … Just think of the air (er, vacuum?) you could catch moon-boarding down the edge of a lunar crater or mountain in such low gravity!

Lots of people think this photo shows Alan Shepard famously hitting a golf ball on the Moon, but it is actually a photo of Apollo 15 crew member James B. Irwin digging a trench on the lunar surface.

Or imagine flying around a lunar sports dome using a glider with wings you can flap. You would be able to take off from the ground using your own muscle power and fly hundreds of feet into the air.

And what would car racing on the Moon look like? At first, the cars might be similar to the open-air buggies that the Apollo astronauts drove across the hills and dunes of the lunar surface. Those buggies had straps to keep you from bouncing out of the vehicle and a joystick for steering (a steering wheel is hard to grasp in a bulky space suit). But with the development of a Moon colony and the need for more surface transportation, buggies might be designed to be smaller and fully enclosed to provide a sealed oxygen environment. (In fact, NASA already has plans for such vehicles.) Eventually, paved lunar roads would enable people to drive around and between lunar cities.

And then why settle for going from point A to point B? There'd be lots of space for car races along the wide-open lunar seas (which are actually the vast ancient lava flows from extinct volcanoes) or around the inside of crater rims. With so little gravity holding them down and an almost total lack of atmosphere to cause drag, vehicles on the Moon could reach close to or even beyond the speed of sound. And if powered by rockets, high-efficiency batteries or even nuclear power, these Moon racers would *destroy* the current land-speed records set on Earth.

NASA's next-generation Lunar Electric Rover is pressurized, has both sleeping and sanitary facilities, and can house two astronauts for up to 14 days.

As part of NASA's Apollo program that ran from 1961 to 1972, 36 astronauts set out on 11 missions orbiting around and later down onto the surface of the Moon. To this day, the Saturn V rockets launched as part of NASA's Apollo Moon program are the tallest, heaviest and most powerful rockets ever flown in space, although both NASA and SpaceX are working on building even larger ships. But not all of NASA's Apollo rockets took people to the Moon. A later version of the Saturn V launcher became Skylab — a research station with more space in one room (about as much as a small restaurant) than any other vehicle that launched before or since (even the ISS).

Space Tour Insider

- The "dark side" of the Moon is actually just the side that always faces away from us when we're on Earth. All sides of the moon get equal amounts of sunlight.

- In 2009, frozen water was found at the lunar north and south poles. It could someday be used to provide lunar visitors with drinking water.

- Don't believe anyone who tries to sell you part of the Moon. Since the 1960s, various laws have banned any country or company from owning and selling parts of the Moon.

- Most recently, the cost of traveling to the Moon as a tourist has been estimated at U.S. $100 million, though SpaceX looks like it will charge less for the two space travelers it hopes to send on its Dragon spacecraft.

- The Moon has a smell. Apollo astronauts who have accidentally brought back traces of regolith to their spacecraft said the strange soil smelled like recently fired gunpowder.

- Contrary to what people might have once believed, the Moon is not made of cheese. (Although it would be cool if it was.) Its surface is actually mostly made up of iron, silicon and oxygen. (The Earth's surface is made up of many of these elements as well, but it is constantly changing due to erosion, living organisms and forces that change the positions of the continents, oceans and mountains.)

This panorama of lunar photographs taken in 1972 during the Apollo 17 mission shows lunar rocks, lunar mountains and astronaut Harrison Schmitt making his way back to the lunar rover.

COMETS: Discovering Your Own
SPACE SNOWBALL

■ ■

▶ **Distance from Earth (average):** 150 million to 1 trillion kilometers (93 million to 621 billion miles) or more
▶ **Total trip time:** 1 to 4 years for "Sun-grazing" comets
▶ **When to go:** year-round, beginning approximately 2030

Highlights

▶ be the first to land on a comet you've "discovered"

▶ play in-flight zero-gravity games

▶ get an up-close look at a comet's tail

A nighttime image of Comet Lovejoy near the Earth's horizon, photographed from the ISS.

Like a cosmic peacock in the sky, the gigantic tail of a nearby comet can be bright enough to be seen in the daytime from Earth. And while comets may be the smallest worlds in our solar system, they're also the most numerous. So what if you were to plan a close encounter with a comet? Chances are you'll be the first person to set foot on any you land on — making you a true space "pioneer"!

Before You Go

A comet is basically a big "dirty snowball" made of ice, rock and dust. Most comets orbit so far from the Sun that they can't be seen from Earth. But when a comet makes its way to the inner solar system (near the orbit of Mars), it's close enough to the Sun for ice in the comet to heat up and vaporize. This produces a tail of water vapor and gas, which can look two, three, even four times the diameter of the full Moon when seen from Earth.

Although the thought of flying through the tail of an active comet might sound cool, it could go down in history as the worst idea ever. Why? When a comet gets close to the Sun, it becomes exposed to high-energy radiation. Contact with these high-energy particles causes gas and dust trapped in the comet's ice to fly away. In some cases, this can trigger geysers to erupt and can even result in part (or all) of the comet breaking apart. So, the perfect time to land on a comet is actually in the weeks *before* its orbit takes it close enough to the Sun to form its beautiful-but-dangerous-to-approach tail.

Before blasting off from Earth, you'll need to use a telescope to identify a comet that's large enough for a ship to land on — one that is at least about 5 to 10 km (3 to 6 mi.) in diameter.

(Above): Vapor and gas can be seen around a comet that has come close to the Sun.

(Below): This photograph of Halley's Comet nucleus was one of the first ever taken of a comet nucleus, in 1986, by the Giotto spacecraft.

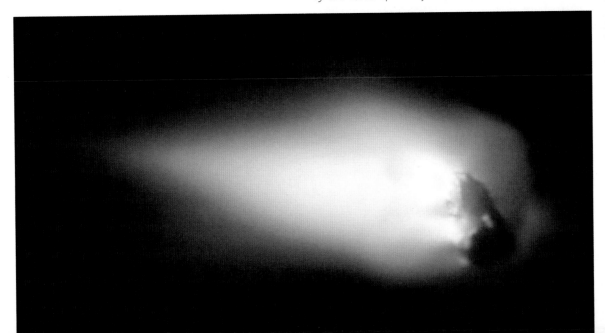

Many space probes have flown by, orbited and even landed on comets. What they've found is stranger than any science-fiction story: dark, jagged features alongside spongy-looking surfaces of rock and water-ice, poisonous chemicals like arsenic, and a mix of organic material that could have given rise to life on Earth. In fact, some scientists believe comets that hit the Earth in the prehistoric past could have deposited the material necessary for life on our home planet.

Your Flight

To reach your comet, you'll need a spacecraft that can achieve incredible speeds: on average, comets reach velocities of about 145 000 km/h (90 000 m.p.h.). That's about one-third faster than Earth travels around the Sun.

Your ship could be used to land on the surface of the comet or, for added safety, it could be equipped with a smaller lander that separates from the mother ship. Your spaceship should also be equipped with tools to break apart bits of the comet to take back home; containers for keeping your samples frozen and uncontaminated for the rest of the mission; and enough food, clothing and other personal supplies to last until you get back home.

Once you've passed through Earth's orbit and are well into your ultimate extended holiday, you'll have months (maybe even years) of time on your hands on your way to your rendezvous with the comet. This would be a great time to find yourself an out-of-this-world hobby.

For starters, how about making a ginormous Lego creation in one of the zero-g areas of your ship? With almost no chance of having your creation fall apart under its own weight the way it would on

(Top): This image of Comet 67P/Churyumov–Gerasimenko was taken by the ROLIS camera system from about 3 km (1.9 mi.) away during the descent of the Philae lander.

(Bottom): The horizon of Comet 67P/Churyumov–Gerasimenko nucleus appears jagged in this image taken by the navigation camera on the Rosetta spacecraft.

Earth, you could build the craziest designs with gravity-defying arcs, bridges, wings, tails, antennas and more. And in zero-g, you wouldn't have to worry about building a base for your creation: it could just float around, on display. (Of course, you *would* need a sealed bin or pouch to keep loose pieces from floating away.)

Or how about packing a gaming system that allows you to use your body's movements to control the way characters and vehicles float or fly ... while *you're* floating and flying? Or how about toy space drones that you can race *outside* of your comet-bound spaceship? This far up, the sky is no limit!

During a long space mission, the soles of your feet lose their calluses (from not walking on them) while the tops of your feet start to get very rough (from hooking them around doorways to avoid crashing into the opposite wall of a room you're floating into).

— Suni Williams, ISS crew member and NASA astronaut, who has spent more time in space than any woman in history

For longer trips, such as those beyond the inner solar system, your ship could be designed to spin fast enough to simulate Earth's gravity inside. To avoid the dizzying effects of this spinning, your ship would need to be large enough — many hundreds of meters (or yards) in diameter — that it could spin relatively slowly and still produce a pulling sensation toward the "floor."

An artist's impression of the Rosetta spacecraft at Comet 67P/Churyumov–Gerasimenko. (The image is not to scale.)

Your body will go through many changes as it adjusts to weightlessness in zero-g. After a few hours, your spine will decompress from a lifetime of the weight of your body pressing down on it — you'll actually grow *taller* by an inch or so. Fluids in your body will shift upward, causing a bloated chest and puffy face, as well as possibly cause everything from vertigo (dizziness) to lower-than-normal blood pressure. Your eyes will even move around more in their sockets because of the increased pressure inside your skull pressing slightly on the backs of your eyes. This can distort your vision and may even lead to hallucinations. To varying degrees, most astronauts on long-duration trips get used to these side effects within a few days.

When You Get There

Because comets have so little mass, they have very little gravity. That means that lifting off from a comet's surface is no problem, but any small ship landing on one could bounce right back out into space! To prepare for this challenge, your landing ship needs to have special equipment that secures it to the surface: comet landers have harpoons that shoot into the ground to help anchor them, as well as screws on their feet for attaching to the surface.

The first thing you might find surprising is how warm it is ... compared to other places in the solar system, that is. Some comets have been found to be around -70°C (-94°F) — much warmer than most of the moons of the outer solar system planets. Even so, you'll still need to do your exploring in the climate-controlled comfort of your space suit.

Another thing that might surprise you once you land is how dark the ground is.

Although they look gray in pictures, most comets are basically black due to the organic compounds, such as carbon dioxide, on their surfaces.

Each step on the ultra-low-gravity surface of a comet would push you into the air, and you'd have to wait a minute or two to slowly descend back down before taking your next step. In fact, if you jumped too high, you might accidentally escape the comet's gravity and end up in space!

After blasting off from a few weeks of exploring a never-before-explored comet, and once you are safely on your way back to Earth, you might be lucky enough to look back and see in vivid detail the comet's tail forming as it gets closer and closer to the Sun. But you don't want to get too close — to fly through the trail of ice, dust, gas and rock would feel like flying through a hail of bullets (so, *not* a good idea!), but flying near or even alongside the tail would be one of the most spectacular views in the solar system.

In 2012, the European Space Agency probe *Philae* made the first-ever controlled landing on the surface of a comet. The crewless *Philae* touched down on Comet 67P/Churyumov–Gerasimenko, a 6.7 km (4.1 mi.) diameter comet. At first, the probe was returning photos of an eerie-looking wasteland. But then, mission scientists realized the probe had landed at an angle and that its solar panels were in the shadow of a large wall, likely cast by the rim of a small crater. As a result, *Philae* wasn't able to recharge its batteries, and the craft went silent after only a fraction of its expected lifespan.

A still image from an animation of the Philae lander separating from the Rosetta spacecraft to touch down on the surface of Comet 67P/Churyumov–Gerasimenko.

Rosetta *mission poster showing the descent of the* Philae *lander on Comet 67P/Churyumov–Gerasimenko.*

The surface of comets can vary wildly over short distances. When *Philae* landed on the surface of Comet 67P/Churyumov–Gerasimenko, it sent back images of some areas that appeared to be dust covered, while others looked like they were made up of a pitted and likely brittle material. Other areas were rocky, while some were smooth with large depressions. This comet (and possibly others like it) also has a set of features known as "gates": twin, wall-like cliffs rising up from the surface. Comet 67P/Churyumov–Gerasimenko is also incredibly stinky. Not that you should take your space suit helmet off to take a sniff, but if you could, it would probably smell like rotten eggs and horse pee. That's because there are jets of hydrogen sulfide and ammonia gas near the comet's surface. According to one European Space Agency (ESA) official, "If you could smell the comet, you would probably wish that you hadn't."

In 2006, NASA's *Stardust* spacecraft flew very close to Comet Wild 2 and used a robotic collection arm to grab particles of dust streaming from the comet's surface. When samples from *Stardust* returned to Earth, scientists found glycine — one of the basic materials needed for life to form.

An artist's rendering of the Stardust spacecraft during its close encounter with Comet Wild 2.

A section of Comet 67P/Churyumov–Gerasimenko's smaller lobe as seen through Rosetta's camera.

- While a comet nucleus (the solid ball the tail sprouts from) is typically around 5 to 10 km (3 to 6 mi.) in diameter, a comet's tail can stretch longer than the Sun is wide!

- Often most of a comet nucleus's ice is made of water (H_2O), but comets can also contain frozen ammonia (sometimes found in fertilizers), carbon dioxide (the gas you exhale), carbon monoxide (found in car exhaust) and methane (a natural gas that smells like farts).

- Comets sometimes hit Earth. In fact, some scientists believe it was the impact of an icy comet that blew Sun-blocking dust into the air to kill plants, disrupt the food chain and lead to the extinction of the dinosaurs.

- Comets can actually have two tails that can be seen in photos: one made of dust that follows the path of the comet around the Sun (this is the one that you can see with just your naked eye) and one made of gas that points away from the direction of the solar wind.

- Astronomers think that there are hundreds of billions — maybe even trillions — of comets in a "bubble" around the Sun that's *trillions* of kilometers (or miles) wide.

- Humans have only ever witnessed one comet collision. In 1994, telescope and space probe photos showed Comet Shoemaker–Levy 9 hitting Jupiter. A string of black "bruises" was visible for weeks in the cloud tops of our solar system's largest planet.

- The gravity of most comets is less than one thousandth of Earth's.

- Comets have been detected around at least 10 stars other than our Sun.

An image of Comet NEAT captured by the Kitt Peak National Observatory in Arizona in May 2004.

MARS: A Journey to the RED PLANET

- ▶ **Distance from Earth (average):** 225 million km (140 million mi.)
- ▶ **Travel time (one way):** 5 to 10 months
- ▶ **When to go:** once every two years, when Earth and Mars are positioned in their orbits to allow for the shortest trip

Highlights

- ▶ fly through the Mariner Valley
- ▶ climb the tallest mountain on any planet in the solar system
- ▶ stand in the eye of a swirling Martian dust devil

An image of Mars, the Red Planet, taken by NASA's Viking 1 Orbiter. The north polar residual ice cap can be seen at the top.

A trip to Mars would be the ultimate extreme adventure: imagine landing on a planet that has a mountain so huge it dwarfs Mount Everest, planet-wide dust storms and a canyon so long that it can be covered in the dark of night at one end while still getting the afternoon daylight at the other. While no one has visited Mars yet, there have been plans for a mission to the Red Planet since even before the first Moon landings. These plans are now closer to a reality than ever before.

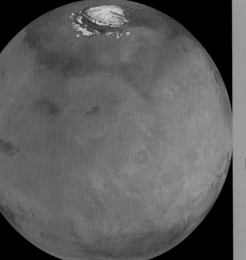

Part of the reason the International Space Station was built was so it could serve as a stepping-stone for travel to Mars. For example, in order to learn more about the needs and challenges experienced by humans on a long trip to Mars, the length of time astronauts live on the ISS has been extended from just three to six months to a full year. As well, NASA's powerful new Space Launch System (SLS) rocket and its Orion crew module have been designed to carry astronauts to Mars, a goal that could be reached in the 2030s or later.

Before You Go

Mars is the fourth planet from the Sun, making it Earth's not-so-close neighbor. It's also the second-smallest planet in the solar system (Mercury is the smallest). Often called the Red Planet, Mars's color is the result of millions of years of iron oxidation (rusting). Like Earth, Mars has two frozen poles at its north and south, but unlike Earth, it has two moons. And although humans can't survive the extreme conditions of Mars without an enormous amount of technology, recently discovered evidence of liquid water on the surface has many scientists wondering if life once existed on the planet.

One way to prepare for a trip to Mars is to train in an Earth environment that is as close to being on the Red Planet as you can get. Small groups of people have lived for months at a time in sealed modules both high in the Canadian Arctic and on a mountain in Hawaii. The cold temperatures (yes, the mountaintops of Hawaii are cold) and low air pressure at these sites provide the best simulations on Earth for training to live in a habitat surrounded by Mars's thin atmosphere. And because of their elevation, these places have levels of solar radiation somewhat similar to that found in some areas of Mars.

Training at these locations includes getting used to living in a small, contained space with only a handful of other people for long periods of time, maintaining science experiments, growing food and keeping detailed mission logs. Trainees only venture outside their modules in "space suits" designed to imitate the experience of being on another planet.

Training camp set up near McMurdo Station in the Antarctic. (Inset): Scientists at the Flashline Mars Arctic Research Station in the Canadian Arctic.

Your Flight

You can't simply fly in a straight line from Earth to Mars. That's because Mars is always moving in its orbit around the Sun. To get to Mars, you'll need to calculate where Mars will be by the time you reach it. In other words, you'll blast off for an area of space *ahead* of where the Red Planet is at the time you leave Earth. The faster your rocket, the shorter the distance ahead of Mars you'll have to aim for and the quicker your trip will be. With today's technology, trips to Mars would take months, but future trips (in the next decade or so) could take as little as 30 days.

To reach Mars, you'll need a rocket with enough power to first break away from the pull of Earth's gravity and then fly millions of kilometers (or miles) into space. On top of that, you'll need a heavy-duty, multi-stage rocket that is large enough to carry people and enough supplies for the lengthy trip. (Large equipment, such as wheeled surface vehicles, and materials to build living quarters would likely be sent ahead of the crew.)

For the comfort of passengers who will need to be on board for many months, your ship could be designed to have an area that simulates Earth's gravity. Ideally, another section would simulate half to one-third Earth's gravity, which can be used to prepare for your time on Mars.

As well as NASA's goal of sending astronauts to Mars, a number of private groups (organizations without ties to a government) have planned to send travelers to the Red Planet, and there's been no shortage of people wanting to jump on board.

In 2012, a mission known as Mars One aimed to send a half-dozen people to Mars for the rest of their lives. That's right: nobody was coming back! Still, thousands of people applied to be crew members. The plan would have involved robot craft dropping supplies in 2020, followed by human volunteers as early as 2024. Funding for the estimated U.S. $6 billlion price tag would have been paid for by broadcasting the mission as a reality series on TV and the internet.

In 2013, space tourist, businessman and former engineer Dennis Tito proposed a mission that would take people on a

This concept image shows the rocket of the SpaceX Interplanetary Transport System making an upright landing upon its return to Earth.

flight past Mars in 2021. Tito and his team aimed to send a crew of two people on a rocket-powered spaceship that would fly by Mars without stopping, using a gravitational "slingshot" around the planet to return to Earth. By flying over Mars's surface at a proposed height of 100 km (60 miles), passengers would get to see Martian craters, mountains, canyons and polar ice caps.

While neither of these early missions were able to find funding, Elon Musk, the founder of the space exploration company SpaceX, is now planning to send up to a dozen people to Mars as early as 2024. For this mission, SpaceX is developing a vehicle called an Interplanetary Transport System (ITS) — an enormous, multi-story, reusable spacecraft launched from atop the largest reusable rocket ever built. The Interplanetary Spaceship is being designed to transport between 100 and 200 people and will likely have movie theaters, lecture halls and a restaurant.

When it launches, the 50 m (160 ft.) tall Interplanetary Spaceship would separate from the 120 m (400 ft.) rocket once reaching Earth orbit. A second rocket would then be sent up to provide more fuel to the Interplanetary Spaceship, which would then fire its engines to break out of orbit and reach Mars within an incredibly fast 80 to 150 days.

Once there, the Interplanetary Spaceship would serve as the "Mars base" for humans while on the surface, before the crew uses it to blast off for their return to Earth. Because Mars has less gravity than Earth, the Interplanetary Spaceship would have enough power to leave the Red Planet without an additional rocket booster.

When You Get There

Landing on Mars will be tough! Mars has a very thin atmosphere. This makes it hard to use friction with the atmosphere to slow a spacecraft down for landing. The thin atmosphere also makes using a parachute to slow down your spaceship less effective. Robotic missions to Mars have also faced challenges with computer glitches, communications problems and bad weather.

But once you've landed and adjusted to the time delay when communicating with Earth (anywhere from 3 to 22 minutes, depending on where Mars is in its orbit), the need for space suits and the realization that there is no way to quickly return home in the case of an emergency, you might actually feel more at home on Mars than any other place in the solar system.

For example, the Mars landscape has features that might remind you of Earth: mountains and canyons, as well as some water, ice caps and flat dunes of sand. There's also wind and even storms, although the atmospheric pressure is so low you'd hardly feel the force of any breeze. And like on Earth, there are seasons (although twice as long) and a roughly 24-hour day. There's also sky, although it's a yellow-brown "butterscotch" color instead of blue. And from Mars's surface, the Sun in the sky looks about the same as on Earth, only slightly smaller.

To make the Red Planet habitable for humans, living quarters will likely be made of capsules and other small habitats — specially made buildings that have been shipped from Earth. Buildings will need a thick radiation shield for protection from the Sun's solar flares or they might even be built underground so the Martian soil

acts as a natural radiation shield. (Although it is farther from the Sun than Earth, Mars doesn't have a strong magnetic field protecting it from harmful solar radiation the way Earth does.) Vehicles and clothing would also need to be designed to provide some radiation protection.

Your day might begin with the *beep, beep, beep* of an alarm clock alerting you that it's time to get out of bed, and a quick check of your calendar tells you it's day 628 of the current Martian year. (The Mars year is almost twice the length of a year on Earth due to its larger orbit around the Sun.) It's the end of summer on the Red Planet, but the morning sunrise is still distant and winter-like. When the Sun rises on Mars, it appears slightly blue in a pink-orange morning sky. Grains, plants and perhaps even egg-laying chickens could be farmed by long-term colonists, so you might make your breakfast from food that's been home-grown in giant pressurized domes.

When it's time to go outside, you'll put on your Mars suit — a heavy-duty space suit built for living in low gravity with a much lower air pressure than Earth and no oxygen. At only 38 percent of the gravity of Earth, life on Mars would feel like something between the weightlessness of zero gravity and the 1g you're used to on your home planet.

An artist's concept of a future mission to Mars, showing two explorers, a robotic lander and its small rover.

One day on Mars is roughly 40 minutes longer than Earth's 24-hour day. (Actually, it takes Earth 23 hours, 56 minutes and 4.1 seconds to complete a full rotation, but who's counting?) Some scientists think this small difference could have big effects on humans living on Mars: working on Mars time for just a few months was enough to result in "rocket lag" (instead of jet lag) that exhausted mission control staff working on NASA's Mars rovers. It might even drive some people crazy over long periods.

Things to Do

Live the life of a Martian

As the second-smallest planet in the solar system, Mars has barely a quarter of the surface area that Earth has. But while most of Earth's surface is covered in water, *all* of Mars's surface is solid ground. That means that the Red Planet actually has just as much surface to walk or drive over as Earth. For that reason, you'll want to set aside lots of time to explore Mars's incredible landscape.

How about starting your tour of Mars with a trip to the Red Planet's "Antarctic," which has almost as much frozen water as Greenland's ice sheet. Mars's south pole sometimes gets dry "snow" during the winter and geyser-like carbon dioxide eruptions when temperatures climb in the summer. You might even be able to gather enough frozen CO_2 together to make a "snow Martian." (Don't forget to pack a carrot for the nose.)

Up near the equator, you can visit the final resting place of the first Mars rovers: the radio-controlled, car-sized *Sojourner* that landed in 1996, the golf-cart-sized *Spirit* and *Opportunity* that landed in 2004 and the compact-car-sized *Curiosity* that landed in 2012.

You could also experience the wonders of Martian wind during your stay. While huge, planet-wide dust storms on Mars can occasionally make the stars in the sky hard to see, the much smaller, building-sized dust devils that swirl across the surface are inspiring to watch or even to stand inside. (Because of the low atmospheric pressure on Mars, even the most menacing-looking winds have virtually no force behind them.)

And when darkness descends, how about a little astronomy? Don't forget to look up at the Martian night sky where you can watch the tiny Martian moons, Phobos and Deimos, travel across a background of thousands of distant stars. On the horizon, you might sometimes see the brilliant blue-white "star" of Earth.

A Mountain the Size of a Country

Don't forget to visit what could be the most spectacular sight on Mars. At a height of approximately 25 km (16 mi.) above the surrounding plains, Olympus Mons (Latin for Mount Olympus) is the tallest volcano (and tied for tallest mountain) in the solar system. Olympus Mons is three times the height of Mount Everest, the tallest mountain on Earth.

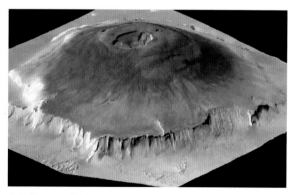

A 3-D view of Olympus Mons.

Olympus Mons has a 624 km (374 mi.) wide caldera (the crater-like center) — a leftover from its days as an active volcano. Its base is so wide that if this shield-shaped volcano were placed on our planet, it would cover most of France.

For sightseers, there's good news and bad news: The good news is that because the slopes of the solar system's tallest volcano are so gentle, you could probably drive right up to the top. The bad news? Because of the huge surface area and shallow slope of Olympus Mons, even if you were on its summit (highest point) it wouldn't feel like you were very high above the ground.

The "Grandest" Canyon

Mars's Mariner Valley is eight times as wide as Earth's Grand Canyon and four times as deep. So standing at the edge of one of this valley's rust-colored cliffs, you might be tempted to look way, waaaaay down to the canyon floor that is 4 km (2 $\frac{1}{2}$ mi.) below.

But don't lean too far over ... that's still quite a fall, even in Mars's low gravity. Plus, things fall five times faster than on Earth. That's because the atmosphere on Mars is so thin that there is little air resistance to slow things down. By the time you landed on the canyon floor, you would be traveling at more than 1000 km/h (600 m.p.h.) — on Earth, that's close to the speed of sound!

And the Mariner Valley is so vast it could take weeks to drive safely end-to-end, along its floor. (It's about the same distance as driving all the way from the east coast to the west coast of North America.) The fastest way to see this continent-sized gash in the side of Mars would be by flying an airborne vehicle above its rocky floor. And what a sight! Imagine watching the crevices, caves and soaring cliff walls zoom by as you fly through this "Grandest Canyon."

This is an image of the Mariner Valley taken by the Mars Odyssey spacecraft, then colored and matched to a computerized topography model to simulate how it would look to the human eye.

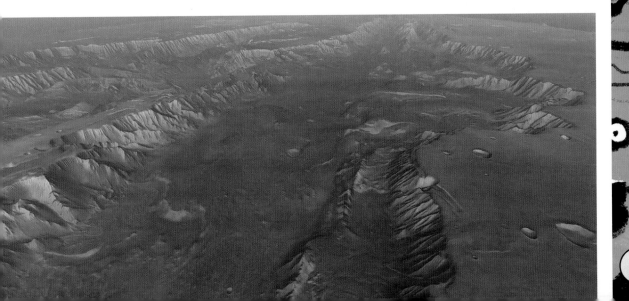

The "Martian Space Program"

Some experts say Mars might one day have its own fleet of rockets for traveling back to Earth or onward to destinations in the outer solar system. According to Space Tourism Society President John Spencer, a Martian space program might even be superior to Earth's one day. For example, because of Mars's lower gravity, spaceships launching from there won't need as much power as rockets that have to escape the Earth's pull. Also, Mars is a much closer jumping-off point to places such as Jupiter, Saturn and their moons.

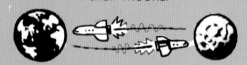

A "Martian space program" is going to kick the Earth space program's butt. It's going to be pretty interesting when we start having people who travel so much between planets, they consider themselves "citizens of the solar system." These people might spend most of their time away from the Earth. Some might even be born in places other than Earth.

– John Spencer, former NASA engineer, president of the Space Tourism Society

Someday we may find alien life on Mars: us. If the plans to send humans to live on the Red Planet come true, those human colonists could be considered "Martians." In fact, eventually citizens of Mars might even develop their own culture and government. Imagine what kind of out-of-this-world art, philosophies, traditions and innovations might be created in a society of humans who are born and live on this alien world.

- Billions of years ago, Mars may have had large oceans of water on its surface, as well as a much thicker atmosphere.

- Sunsets on Mars are blue! On Earth, blue light from the Sun is scattered by molecules in the air and spreads around the sky making it appear blue. Because Mars has less than 1 percent of Earth's atmosphere, we only see the blue light when looking through the thickest part of Martian air and dust on the horizon when the Sun is setting (or rising).

- Humans may not have landed on Mars yet, but our artificial ambassadors have made the journey. Right now, there are several crewless American, European, Russian and Indian spacecraft orbiting Mars, including NASA's *Mars Reconnaissance Orbiter (MRO)* and *Mars Atmosphere and Volatile EvolutioN (MAVEN)*. And maybe even more exciting are the wheeled robotic rovers that have landed on the planet's surface, such as NASA's *Opportunity* and *Curiosity* vehicles.

- The surface of Mars isn't entirely red — it also contains blacks, grays and blues, as well as shades of dark to light rust colors.

- The only thing in the solar system known to be taller than Olympus Mons is Rheasilvia, the escarpment (a kind of big, rocky "shelf") in the middle of a crater on the asteroid Vesta, just beyond Mars. This feature rises almost straight up like a pillar and is a few hundred meters (or yards) taller than Mars's great peak.

(Left): A selfie taken by the Curiosity Mars rover in August 2015.

(Below): This image taken by Curiosity shows a site on Mars with many large mineral deposits in the rock.

JUPITER: A Solar System Within a SOLAR SYSTEM

- **Distance from Earth (average):** 800 million kilometers (497 million miles)
- **Travel time (one way):** 3 to 5 years
- **When to go:** year-round, beginning approximately 2050

Highlights

- watch the spinning clouds of the Great Red Spot, our solar system's largest storm

- see a volcano erupt on the moon Io

- ice skate on the frozen water of the moon Europa

- witness the largest, most powerful auroras in the solar system

Less than 50 years ago, taking a plane was a big deal. So just imagine how travel technology will change and advance in the next 50 years or so. By then, an outer solar system adventure to Jupiter — a world so huge that it could fit 1300 Earths inside it — could be possible. A trip to this gas giant, where a cloud can be larger than the entire Earth and lightning flashes can stretch longer than a country, is what space adventuring is all about.

Before You Go

Beyond Mars and the asteroid belt lies the outer solar system, which includes the gas giant planets: Jupiter, Saturn, Uranus and Neptune. Gas giants are basically huge ball-shaped clouds, with no solid surfaces for landing on.

Jupiter is the fifth and largest planet in the solar system. It's also the stormiest. It and its dozens of moons are sometimes called the Jovian system, a miniature solar system within our own. Io, Europa, Ganymede and Callisto are Jupiter's largest moons. These four moons are the size of planets and are sometimes called the Galilean satellites after Galileo Galilei (1564–1642), the scientist who discovered them in 1610.

It won't be a short or necessarily safe trip for an outer solar system space adventurer: in addition to the obvious dangers of solar and cosmic radiation exposure, people on long spaceflights face many other challenges, including dramatic muscle loss and bone loss (called osteoporosis) that happens when you're living in zero gravity for months or years at a time. Scientists think bone loss happens because bones aren't under the same kind of pressure as they are on Earth. So having a ship (or at least a part of it) that has a spinning gravity simulator to keep you at an Earth-like 1g would

be extremely important. (Looking out the window for the first few days may make you feel pretty sick to your stomach, but it sure beats wasting away from osteoporosis.)

For successful trips to the outer solar system, spaceship engines will need to be more efficient; advanced materials for strong radiation shields made out of thin, lightweight materials will need to be developed; and more efficient ways to recycle water, food and electronics will need to be created. And a trip from Earth to Jupiter would take several times longer than a voyage to Mars. That means that even once the technology is available, travel to the outer planets will be extremely expensive, require lots of time, and passengers will need to be in excellent physical and mental health. Think you're up for it?

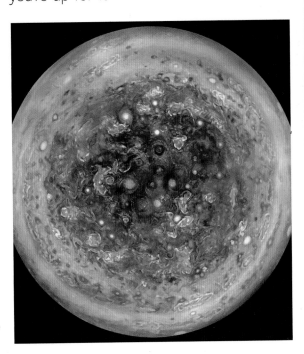

Jupiter's south pole, as seen by the Juno spacecraft from an altitude of 52 000 km (32 000 miles). The oval forms are cyclones.

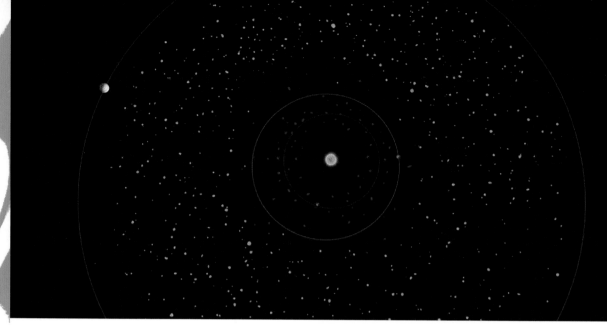

This diagram shows a bird's-eye view of the asteroid belt. The purple, red and blue circles represent the orbits of Jupiter, Mars and Earth, respectively.

Your Flight

To reach orbit around Jupiter and its moons, your rocket will have to pass through the millions of asteroids that make up the asteroid belt that lies between Mars and Jupiter. But don't worry: the asteroids are so far apart that spacecraft have been traveling through this region without incident for decades.

When you do finally reach your destination after your years-long flight, it will probably feel less like an "ahhh ..." moment and more like an "aaaagh!" That's because your ship will likely use Jupiter's gravity and thick atmosphere to slow it down enough to enter orbit. (Remember, Jupiter is a gas giant and doesn't have a solid surface to land on.)

Skimming along Jupiter's upper atmosphere, your ship will pile on as many as 9 gs of force. During this time, you'll face the overwhelming effects of high gs, such as tunnel vision, loss of vision and even temporary loss of consciousness. To help you deal with these unpleasant side effects, you'll need to wear a next-generation g-suit.

You'll also have been trained in special exercises that will help you stay conscious. Basically, you repeatedly clench your arm and leg muscles as tightly as you can and then release, all while making grunting sounds like the "hut" noise a football player makes before snapping a football. This helps keep blood circulating rather than pooling in the lower part of your body, and reduces your chance of blacking out until the g-forces finally ease up.

From the first day you arrive in space, you are literally peeing out your skeleton [from bone loss due to lack of gravity].

— Chris Hadfield, Canadian astronaut, International Space Station Expedition 35 commander

Sailing out of sight of land, early automobiles, early aviation ... initially, there was a lot of research, a lot of dead ends, risks and problems. Those experiences [at first] weren't available to the common person at all ... Today, we complain if our movie or internet access is interrupted briefly on a flight.

— Chris Hadfield, Canadian astronaut, International Space Station Expedition 35 commander

Until the technology to make spacecraft engines more efficient takes a giant leap forward, long-haul spaceships won't be able to carry enough fuel to slow themselves down (in other words, "put on the brakes") when entering orbit around Jupiter's massive gravity field. With today's technology, a ship would need to use the atmosphere of the planet to slow it down and settle into orbit. This saves on fuel needed for the trip back to Earth, but it also makes for a *very* bumpy ride!

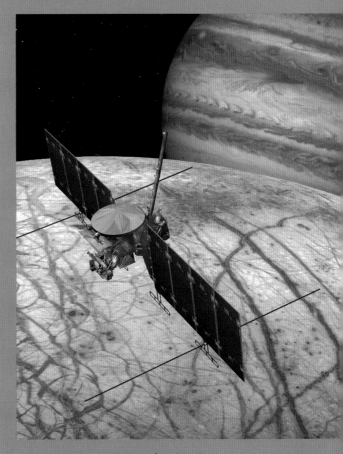

This is an artist's rendering of NASA's Europa mission spacecraft, which is being developed for a launch in the 2020s.

Things to Do

Looking down from Jupiter's orbit, you'll see the gas giant's red, orange, brown, beige and white clouds moving in swirls and ripples as huge bands of gas circle the planet. And once you've recovered from the experience of getting into a stable orbit and confirmed your ship's radiation shield is protecting you from the gas giant's magnetic field, you can prepare to experience a mini solar system's worth of wonders.

Jupiter's most famous feature is the Great Red Spot — a swirling 300-year-old storm that's large enough to fit two Earths inside it. The "spot" varies in color from dark red to light red to white, when it then seems to "disappear" and leave what looks like a hole in the clouds around the planet.

The Great Red Spot makes one full, counter-clockwise rotation every six Earth days. Watching this titanic storm out your spaceship window would be one of the most mesmerizing experiences of your trip. So much so that you might be tempted to travel closer for a better view. But don't! Too close and your radiation shield would eventually be ineffective, and you'd get zapped by Jupiter's intense radiation and crushed by its immense gravity.

For a safer up-close-and-personal experience, you've got your pick of Jupiter's 69 moons (at last count) to land on and explore. Here are some suggestions:

A close-up of swirling clouds around the Great Red Spot taken by the Voyager 1 spacecraft in 1979.

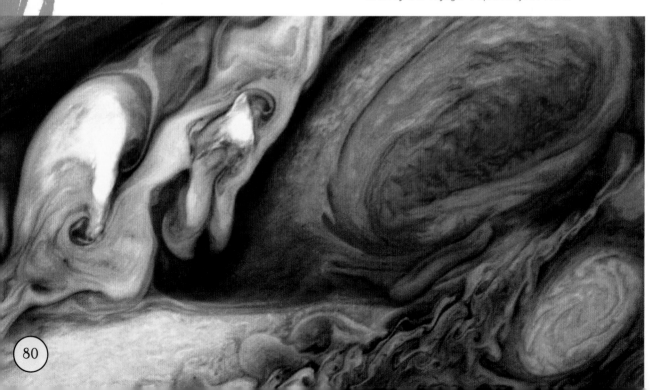

▶ Ganymede — The largest of Jupiter's four Galilean moons, Ganymede is also the largest moon in the solar system. Recently, scientists detected the presence of a large saltwater ocean under Ganymede's surface — imagine the possibility of taking a submarine voyage under the waters of an alien moon!

▶ Callisto — This is the third-largest moon in the solar system, and it is also the oldest and most cratered. From here, you could take in a distant view of Jupiter and its many other moons. After that, you could visit this moon's awe-inspiring ice-spires — a series of 80 to 100 m (260 to 330 ft.) high towers of ice and dust. These spires are actually eroding away, even though little else on this ancient world has changed in billions of years.

▶ Io — The most explosive moon in the solar system, Io has over 400 active volcanoes shooting sulfur more than 500 km (310 mi.) into space. Beautiful plumes of exploding chemicals make Io one of the most colorful places in the solar system (and the most stinky — sulfur smells like rotten eggs). Scientists believe this moon actually turns itself inside out every million years or so because of its volcanic activity.

▶ Europa — This moon's entire surface is covered in water. Other than Earth, Europa is the only place in the solar system known to have so much of the life-giving liquid covering its surface. However, because of its vast distance from the Sun, all the water on Europa's surface appears to be frozen solid. Still, many scientists believe there is a giant ocean below the ice, heated by the gravitational tug-of-war between Europa, the other moons and Jupiter. Vacation plans on Europa could range from ice-skating to discovering a new form of life in what could be the solar system's largest underground body of water.

▶ Metis — Scientists believe this tiny, potato-shaped world is Jupiter's closest moon. Your view of the sky from the surface of this 50 km (30 mi.) wide rock would be filled mostly with Jupiter. From here, you could see the awesome details of Jupiter's swirling cyclones; the planet's fierce lightning; and Jupiter's rivers of gaseous clouds longer than the distance between Earth and our Moon. Make sure you've got a good pair of sunglasses, though: Jupiter may be more than five times farther from the Sun than Earth, but at 1300 times the volume of Earth, that's a lot of planet to reflect the Sun's light!

Astronomers are able to study Jupiter's auroras by using the Hubble Space Telescope's ultraviolet capabilities, as seen in this image.

▶ Last but definitely not least, another spectacular sight to check out is the gas giant's powerful auroras. Like the Earth's Northern and Southern lights, these beautiful light displays sometimes swirl around Jupiter's north and south poles when energetic particles interact with the planet's magnetic field. But unlike the lights that only sometimes appear above Earth, Jupiter's auroras are a permanent feature and are actually made from the energetic particles of erupting volcanoes on the moon Io. Once ejected into space, these particles are drawn into Jupiter's magnetic field. Because Jupiter's magnetic field is many times more powerful than that of any other planet in our solar system, auroras here can be dozens of times bigger than those seen on Earth.

Space Tour Insider

- NASA's *Juno* spacecraft is the second robot probe to go into orbit around Jupiter. Starting in 2016, the mission has so far revealed that Jupiter's north and south poles are full of gray-black clouds, which are completely different from the white, beige, brown, orange and red clouds around the rest of the gas planet.

- Like the other gas planets, Jupiter has a system of rings around it. But unlike Saturn's rings, Jupiter's rings are only visible using the high-resolution cameras of spacecraft. In fact, Jupiter's rings were only discovered in 1979 by NASA's *Voyager 1* spacecraft as it flew by the planet.

- Jupiter is so massive that it doesn't actually orbit around the Sun — the Sun and Jupiter orbit around *each other*. The Sun wobbles a tiny bit as Jupiter circles it, with the center of gravity between the two being just above the surface of the Sun.

- Jupiter rotates much faster than Earth. Its whirling speed causes it to visibly bulge at its equator. It also means that a day on the gas giant is only 10 hours long.

- While Jupiter is about -150°C (-300°F) at its cloud tops, a little farther down, temperatures can get hotter than the boiling point of water.

- Jupiter's moon Ganymede is the only satellite known to have its own magnetic field. This means that Ganymede is also the only moon to have auroras.

- Callisto has a 1600 km (995 mi.) wide crater called Asgard, named after the home of the mythical Norse gods of the Vikings.

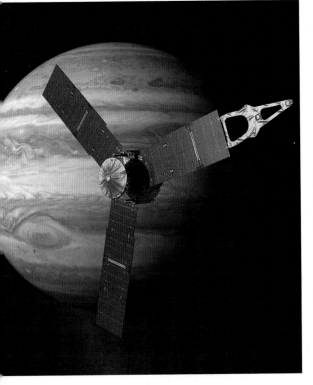

(Left): An artist's concept of the Juno mission to Jupiter.

(Right): This image of Jupiter's north polar region was taken by the Juno spacecraft as it approached the planet in August 2016.

SATURN: A Frozen PARADISE

- ▶ **Distance from Earth (average):** 1.4 billion km (870 billion mi.)
- ▶ **Travel time (one way):** 6 to 7 years
- ▶ **When to go:** year-round, beginning approximately 2070

Highlights

- ▶ take a spacewalk through one of Saturn's rings
- ▶ set sail on the super-moon Titan
- ▶ check out ice volcanoes on the moon Enceladus

Most famous for the rings that circle it, the gas giant Saturn is often considered the most beautiful sight in the solar system. As the widest planet (if you include its rings) in the solar system and one big enough to hold 800 Earths, there's no shortage of places to explore. Oh, and did we mention it has over 60 moons to check out, too?

Before You Go

Saturn is the sixth planet from the Sun and the so-called "Lord of the Rings." The other gas giants have rings, too, but Saturn's are the largest and brightest — you can see these rings from Earth using a telescope or even powerful binoculars. Amazingly, though, the rings are also very thin — only about a kilometer (a little over half a mile) thick at most.

At their widest diameter, Saturn's main rings are more than 300 000 km (186 000 mi.) across — that's almost the distance between Earth and the Moon. There are seven main rings (each named after a letter of the alphabet from A to G) with many, many smaller rings within the larger rings and others stretching millions of kilometers (or miles) beyond.

According to France's International Space University (whose staff includes astronauts, engineers and leaders from NASA and other space agencies), the first mission to the outer planets that will include humans (not just probes that send information back to Earth) is likely to depart sometime after 2050.

The Cassini spacecraft took this magnificent image of Saturn while looking back toward the eclipsed Sun from within the shadow of the planet.

Your Flight

A flight to the ringed planet will take around seven years one-way. Crewless robot space probes have made the trip in faster time, though. Why is there such a range in how long it can take? It all depends on the kind of trip.

On its way to the outer solar system, NASA's *Voyager 1* spacecraft took just three years to do a flyby of Saturn (meaning a flight past the planet without stopping to orbit around it.) On the other hand, NASA's *Cassini* spacecraft took almost seven years to make the trip before it slowed down to enter orbit around the ringed planet.

Cassini carried just enough fuel to fire the rockets that slowed it down enough to be captured by Saturn's gravity and enter the gas giant's orbit. The length of time *Cassini*'s trip took is likely similar to what a human visit to Saturn would involve.

Vessels for long-duration missions to the outer solar system planets will probably be designed to be more like the massive International Space Station than a rocket or space shuttle. As multi-module ships, they would have room for you to stretch out, exercise and partake in your favorite games and hobbies in order to pass the time. (Did we mention it would take years to get there?)

An artist's rendering of the Cassini *spacecraft orbiting Saturn in the Cassini–Huygens mission.*

When you're this far from home, you'll need everything instantly available on one ship (unlike a trip to closer Mars, no supplies will have been sent ahead of you). And your ship will need to be big enough to have its own artificial-gravity area to prevent the long-term bone and muscle loss that humans experience in zero gravity. The ship could include a room with sunlamps and plants (which might also be a food source) to keep you from missing life on Earth too much. And, of course, there also needs to be room on the ship for all the vehicles and large equipment being transported, such as landers, probes, tools, sample collection gear, escape craft and robots for maintenance and leisure.

As an added step to keeping sane on your long trip, you might decide to stay on a 24-hour day aboard your ship. This way you can maintain your body's natural rhythms, even though you may not see all the sunsets and sunrises you're used to for years. Or you could even choose to be put into a state of artificial "hibernation" to sleep your way to — and maybe also from — your destination.

Once you finally arrive, you'll need to watch out: entering orbit around Saturn or its moons can be a real traffic jam. There are trillions of particles that make up each of Saturn's many rings. To avoid your ship being damaged by ring fragments, you will need to approach Saturn from either above or below the rings.

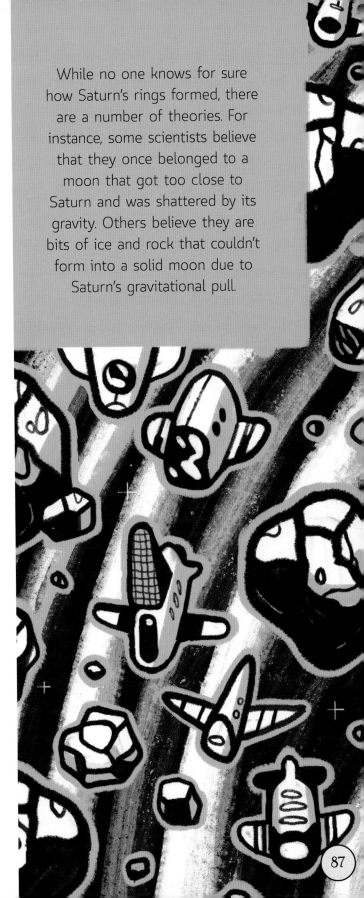

While no one knows for sure how Saturn's rings formed, there are a number of theories. For instance, some scientists believe that they once belonged to a moon that got too close to Saturn and was shattered by its gravity. Others believe they are bits of ice and rock that couldn't form into a solid moon due to Saturn's gravitational pull.

In theory, long-duration space travelers journeying to places like the outer planets could be put into a state of hibernation, much like how an animal goes into a deep sleep over the winter. While science fiction often suggests this could be done by "freezing" the travelers, a more probable way to do this could be to drain their blood and quickly replace it with a low-temperature solution that slows down all their bodily processes. This technique has already been tested safely in animals that were able to "hibernate" for up to three hours. In the future, this technique could be perfected for use on humans for periods of years.

The most fun I had while I was in space was definitely spacewalking. You're not just stuck on the glass-bottom boat [of your vessel] with windows facing Earth: you can turn around and go anywhere.

— Suni Williams, ISS crew member and NASA astronaut

Things to Do

Even though you can't set foot on Saturn itself, there's no shortage of places for you to orbit around, fly past and touch down on.

"Walking" Among the Rings of Saturn

One of the most awe-inspiring space adventures you might one day have is to take a space walk through one of the main rings of Saturn. Of course, the trillions of particles that make up the rings would make it less of a walk and more of an extreme sport — most of these particles are gravel-sized but some can be the size of a bus, all traveling at thousands of kilometers (or miles) an hour. To approach the rings, you'll need to travel cautiously using a smaller ship launched from your main spacecraft (making it easier to navigate through the debris) and moving at the same velocity as the ring particles.

Imagine what a space walk out here would be like — just you alone, decked out in the latest-model space suit that acts as your own personal, form-fitting spaceship, while you float out in space among trillions of particles of ice that gleam in the distant sunlight.

A close-up illustration of the particles that make up Saturn's vast system of rings.

Ringside Seats

By flying your ship a few thousand kilometers (or miles) above the rings, you'll have a spectacular view of the thousands of strands of debris that make up the rings. From even farther away, you could travel to the "dark side" of the planet and view the full extent of the rings as the light of the Sun illuminates them from behind.

Another sight not to be missed is Saturn's striking auroras. Dozens of times the size of Earth, these blue-green halos of light stand out against the light beige of the planet's cloud tops. Imagine floating above these majestic rippling lights for the day or so it would take your spaceship to travel past them.

Approaching either one of Saturn's poles on the way to see these auroras, you'll also be able to watch the high winds whip Earth-sized clouds around the planet's equator at speeds faster than winds almost anywhere else in the solar system.

(Top): An image of a scan across Saturn's many ice rings taken by the Cassini spacecraft.

(Below): This huge storm in Saturn's northern hemisphere, which began in December 2010, is the largest and most intense storm observed on Saturn by the Cassini spacecraft. The storm's tail of clouds encircles the entire planet.

Cowabunga, Dude!

After passing through the heavy clouds of Saturn's super-satellite Titan, you'll find a solid surface you can land on and explore. Titan is Saturn's biggest moon and the second-biggest in the solar system. It has rivers and seas the size of North America's Great Lakes. Here, though, seas are made of methane (that stinky stuff in swamps) and liquid hydrocarbons (similar to elements of the crude oil used to make car fuel). You could swim on Titan, but it would require a thick wetsuit full of air to keep you from sinking: the liquid methane of Titan's lakes and seas has less than half the density of water.

As the only moon in the solar system known to have an atmosphere, Titan is very windy. In its thick atmosphere, even a low-speed wind would push you along with the force of a tidal wave. What's more, because gravity is lower here — only about one-seventh that of Earth's — the wind would blow any object (like a sailboat) faster and farther than if you were on Earth.

So, for a once-in-a-lifetime windsurfing experience, you'll just want to have a windsurf board that can stand up to serious cold. Oh, and a space suit flexible enough for riding the wind, equipped with oxygen and insulated to keep you warm in a place where the average temperature is −170°C (−274°F). Hold on tight!

This image of Titan's surface below its thick clouds is a composite of several images taken by the Cassini *spacecraft.*

Saturn Side-Trips

While orbiting Saturn, you might have a chance to go on a few quick day trips to some of the other 60-plus moons of Saturn:

▶ Mimas — This moon has a giant crater with a mountain in the middle, making it look something like the planet-blasting Death Star spacecraft from *Star Wars*.

▶ Iapatus — This moon is white as snow on one side and dark as ash on the other, maybe as a result of a massive collision with another moon, comet or asteroid during its early history. It also has a huge Great Wall of China–like ridge running along its equator.

▶ Enceladus — One of the most amazing sights in the outer solar system might be the erupting geysers on this tiny 500 km (310 mi.) wide world. Scientists have recently found that the icy spray shooting into space might hold evidence of the conditions needed for life.

▶ Phoebe — This moon is believed to be an icy world captured into orbit by the force of Saturn's gravity. Phoebe's orbit extends outward roughly 150 times Saturn's diameter, just inside a huge but almost invisible part of Saturn's rings.

Looking for Life

It just might be a space tourist (or "citizen scientist") visiting Mars, Europa, Enceladus or maybe Titan who finds evidence of what pre-prehistoric Earth might have been like. In 2010, researchers added energy to a combination of gases like those found in Titan's atmosphere. Amazingly, they discovered complex molecules similar to those needed for making DNA, or the genetic "building blocks" of life. Could life — even in the form of tiny bacteria or single-celled organisms — be possible on this world? If so, it could make Titan the most important place outside Earth for understanding the beginnings of life as we know it.

(Above): This colored radar image of Titan shows two of its largest seas and nearby lakes.

(Top): A montage created from images taken by the Voyager 1 spacecraft of Saturn and six of its moons.

- Although thicker, Titan's atmosphere is more similar to Earth's than any other in the solar system. Even so, at 98 percent nitrogen and almost 2 percent methane, humans would not be able to live here. The air (or atmosphere) we breathe on Earth is 21 percent oxygen, 78 percent nitrogen and about 1 percent miscellaneous elements.

- NASA's *Cassini* spacecraft orbited Saturn, photographing its rings and moons from 2004–2017. When it arrived at Saturn, *Cassini* deployed a lander to explore Titan's surface.

- An average cubic meter (or yard) of Saturn is less dense than water. If you had a lake big enough, it would float.

- Some scientists believe that Saturn's moon Rhea may have its own rings. If so, it would be the only known moon with rings.

- Some of Saturn's moons orbit within the rings. These "shepherd moons" help shape the rings, giving them clear edges and creating some of the gaps between the rings.

Whats Next?
TO THE STARS!

Just a few decades ago, no one knew for sure if there *were* planets beyond our solar system. Today, we know there are *thousands*, including Proxima b, which revolves around Proxima Centauri, the star closest to our Sun.

Because it's slightly more massive than Earth with a bit more gravity, Proxima b is known as a "super Earth." Proxima b is in what scientists call the "Goldilocks zone" around its star. That's an area not too hot or too cold but *juuuust* right. While intense solar radiation may have blasted away Proxima b's atmosphere, there's also a chance liquid water (and life) can exist there. Sounds like it could be an interesting place to visit, right?

Except that at 4 light-years away from Earth, it would take the fastest spacecraft we currently have about *80 000 years* to arrive at Proxima b.

Trying to solve this problem, a team of scientists (with a board of advisers that includes famed scientist Stephen Hawking and Facebook founder Mark Zuckerberg) has come up with a plan to be carried out over the next few decades: to build crewless spaceships the size of postage stamps that could be pushed to the next star by giant lasers. These micro-probes could reach one-fifth the speed of light and make the trip from Earth to Proxima b in only *20* years. Maybe one day this technology could be used to propel ships large enough to carry people.

We're also finding out that planets the size of Earth are likely a common thing outside our solar system. For instance, in 2017, scientists using huge and very powerful telescopes in Chile's Atacama Desert discovered *seven* Earth-sized planets, all in the same star system. Roughly 40 light years away, the planets of TRAPPIST-1 (named after the telescope that first discovered the system) orbit a small red dwarf star about the size of Jupiter but much more massive. Three of the planets in this system are within its Goldilocks zone.

But before you start planning your trip there, you'll need to find a way to attain some truly record-breaking speeds. To get to TRAPPIST-1 in less than a human lifetime, you would need to travel pretty close to the speed of light. Even if we had that technology, weird things happen as you approach such speeds: Your surroundings start to bend, and objects nearby change color. Even weirder, time *outside* your spaceship seems to pass more slowly than inside it.

That means by traveling at 90 percent of the speed of light, your journey to TRAPPIST-1 would take 44 Earth years, although from *your* perspective only 19 years would pass. After a short stay in this alien star system, your trip there and back will feel like about 38 years for you, but almost 100 years will have passed on Earth. The home you return to will be almost a century in the future compared to when you left it. Maybe after all your many travels, *this* will be the ultimate space adventure.

An artist's concept of the surface of one of the planets in the TRAPPIST-1 system.

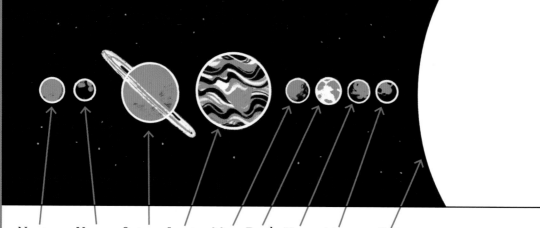

Neptune Uranus Saturn Jupiter Mars Earth Venus Mercury Sun

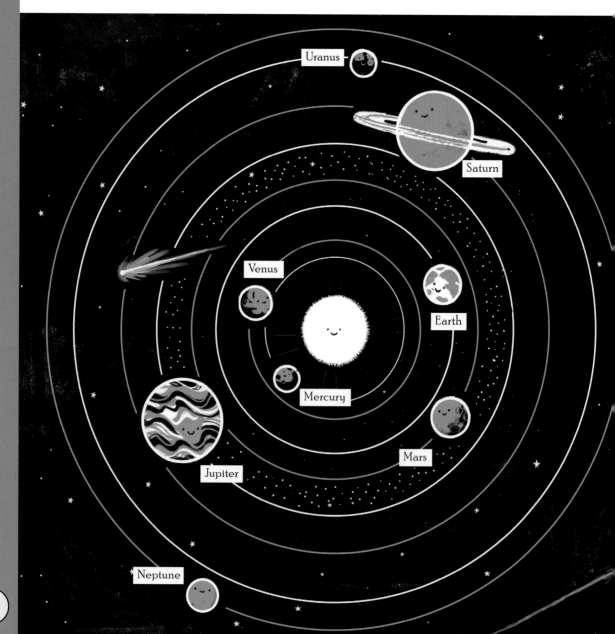